Finance Basics
for Tough Times

Finance Basics for Tough Times

Harvard Business Press

Boston, Massachusetts

Content in this book was previously published in *Understanding Finance*, *Preparing a Budget*, and *Creating a Business Plan* © Harvard Business School Publishing, 2007–2009

Library of Congress Cataloging-in-Publication Data
Finance basics for tough times.
    p. cm. — (Skills you need right now)
 ISBN 978-1-4221-2967-8 (pbk.)
 1. Finance, Personal.
 HG179.F456 2009
 658.15—dc22
                    2009010517

The paper used in this publication meets the requirements of the American National Standard for Permanence of Paper for Publications and Documents in Libraries and Archives Z39.48-1992.

Contents

Introduction

In a downturn, no matter where you work in your organization, understanding basic financial concepts will help you do your job better and contribute to your company's efforts to stay in business and keep turning a profit. Companies are now focused more than ever on the numbers as they try to stay afloat—and the faster you can become literate in financial terms and begin contributing to conversations about the bottom line, the faster you'll be able to help your team.

This book explains the basics of this important subject. In Part I we look at business finance as a whole, and then in Part II we shine a spotlight on budgeting in particular. This volume will not make you a finance expert, nor will it qualify you to become a financial analyst, controller, or CFO. But it *will* explain what you need to know to be an intelligent consumer of financial information, to plan, and to use financial concepts in making business decisions.

Reduced to its essentials, business finance is about acquiring and allocating the resources a company needs to operate. Regarding resource *acquisition*, finance is concerned with questions such as:

- How will our company acquire and finance its inventory, equipment, and other physical assets?

- Should we use the owners' money, borrowed funds, or internally generated cash for resource acquisitions?

- How long does it take to collect money owed to us by customers?

And regarding resource *allocation*, finance helps managers answer questions like:

- If we could invest in several ventures, how might we determine which would ultimately generate the greatest value?

- What return must an investment produce to be worth making? And how should we measure return?

- How can we determine the profitability of our company's different offerings?

Planning for the acquisition and allocation of assets—creating a financial blueprint for action—is the heart of budgeting. In Part II of this volume, we'll explore the benefits of budgeting, examine the various types of budgets and approaches to budgeting, and explore ways to categorize expenses—a key element in preparing a budget. Then you'll discover practical steps for preparing both operating and capital budgets and for deciding how to respond if your department's actual business results don't match what was reflected in your budget.

With the skills you'll learn in this volume under your belt, you'll be ready to understand and tackle many of the challenges your company faces in today's tough economic times.

Understanding Finance

Understanding Financial Statements

But it is pretty to see what money can do.
—Samuel Pepys

COMPANIES DO many things: build cars, process data, provide services, and even launch satellites. But the underlying purpose of all for-profit companies is to make money. As a for-profit manager, your job is to help the company make money—preferably, more money each year. Even if you work in the nonprofit or government sectors, where net income is neither the only nor the most important bottom line, it is still vital that you carefully monitor how much money comes in and where it gets spent.

You can help your company make money by reducing costs, increasing revenues, or both. You can also help the organization be financially successful by making good investments and using its assets to their fullest extent. The best managers don't just mind the budget—they look for the right combination of controlling costs, improving sales, and utilizing assets.

How's your company's financial health? Where does its revenue come from, and where does it spend its money? How much profit is it making? Where is its cash coming from, and where is it going to? Companies provide answers to such questions in three documents, called *financial statements*: the income statement, the balance sheet, and the cash flow statement. Publicly traded companies make these statements available to everyone—shareholders, industry analysts, and competitors as well. As a result, they are not as detailed as the company's internal financial statements.

Accounting methods

Financial statements follow the same general format from company to company. Depending on the nature of the company's business, however, specific line items may vary. Still, the statements are usually similar enough to allow you to compare one business's performance against another's. The reason for this similarity is that accountants abide by *generally accepted accounting principles*, or GAAP.

Most companies use *accrual accounting*: revenue and expenses are booked when they are incurred, regardless of when they are actually received or paid. This system relies on the matching principle, which helps companies understand the true causes and effects of business activities. Accordingly:

- Revenues are recognized during the period in which the sales activity occurred.

- Expenses are recognized in the same period as their associated revenues.

For example, at Amalgamated Hat Rack Company, which manufactures hat racks from imitation moose antlers, the revenue for a customer order is booked when each hat rack is sold—even if payment is made on account and the cash is not received immediately. Similarly, if Amalgamated receives two thousand brass hooks from a contracted supply company, those hooks are not all expensed at once. Rather, they are expensed on a per-unit basis: if it takes five brass hooks to make one hat rack, then the brass hooks are expensed five at a time as each hat rack is sold.

Occasionally, a very small company will begin its existence using *cash-basis accounting*, which counts transactions when cash actually changes hands. This practice is less conservative when it comes to expense recognition, but sometimes more conservative when it comes to revenue recognition. But as companies increase in size and complexity, it becomes more important to match revenues and expenses in the appropriate time periods, so they tend to switch over to accrual accounting.

The income statement

You might want to invest in a company for many reasons. Perhaps it's a leader in the industry. Or its CEO has a great record of turning companies around. Or its products are on the cutting edge of technology. But if the company is not turning a profit (otherwise known as net income or earnings), or it doesn't show strong potential to become profitable over the medium term, you probably wouldn't want to invest in it.

The *income statement* tells you whether the company is making a profit—that is, whether it has positive net income. (This is why the income statement is also called a profit and loss statement.) It shows a company's profitability for a specific period of time—typically, monthly, quarterly, and annually.

How does an income statement present this profitability picture? It starts with a company's revenue: how much money has come in the door from its operations. Various costs—from the costs of making and storing its goods, to depreciation of plant and equipment, to interest and taxes—are then subtracted from the revenue. The bottom line—what's left over—is the *net income* or profit.

Consider the example shown in the table "Income statement for Amalgamated Hat Rack." (Explanations for key terms follow.)

Income statement for Amalgamated Hat Rack

Retail sales	$2,200,000
Corporate sales	$1,000,000
Total revenue	**$3,200,000**
Cost of goods sold	$(1,600,000)
Gross profit	**$1,600,000**
Operating expenses	$(800,000)
Depreciation expense	$(42,500)
Operating income **(also called earnings before interest and taxes)**	**$ 757,500**
Interest expense	$(110,000)
Earnings before income tax	**$647,500**
Income tax	$(300,000)
Net income	**$347,500**

Source: Harvard ManageMentor® on Finance Essentials, adapted with permission.

The *cost of goods sold* is what it cost Amalgamated to manufacture the hat racks. It includes raw materials, such as fiberglass, as well as direct labor costs.

By subtracting the cost of goods sold from revenue, you get a company's *gross profit*—the profitability of the company's products or services.

Operating expenses include administrative employee salaries, rents, sales and marketing costs, as well as other costs of business not directly attributed to manufacturing a product. The fiberglass for making hat racks would not be included here; the cost of the advertising would.

Depreciation is a way of estimating the "consumption" of an asset over time. A computer, for example, might have a useful life of three years. Thus, according to the matching principle, the company would not expense the full value of the computer all in the first year of its purchase, but as it is actually used over a span of three years.

By subtracting operating expenses and depreciation from gross profit, you get *operating income*—often called *earnings before interest and taxes*, or *EBIT*.

Interest expense refers to the interest charged on loans a company takes out.

Income tax is levied by the government on corporate income.

BOTTOM LINE *n* **1:** net income (or profit), as shown on a company's income statement

---

The balance sheet

Most people go to a doctor once a year to get a checkup—a snapshot of their physical well-being at a particular time. Similarly, companies prepare *balance sheets* as a means of summarizing their financial positions at a given point in time.

Assets = liabilities + owners' equity

Assets are the things a company invests in so that it can conduct business—examples include financial instruments, land, buildings, and equipment. In order to acquire necessary assets, a company often borrows money from others or makes promises to pay others. That money, which is owed to creditors, is called *liabilities*. *Owners' equity*, also known as shareholders' equity, includes the capital that investors have provided and the profits retained by the company over time. If a company has $3 million in assets and $2 million in liabilities, it would have owners' equity of $1 million.

Assets	=	**Liabilities**	+	**Owners' equity**
$3,000,000	=	$2,000,000	+	$1,000,000

By contrast, a company with $3 million in assets and $4 million in liabilities would have negative equity of $1 million—and serious problems as well.

Thus, the balance sheet provides a description of how much, and where, the company has invested (its assets)—broken down into how much of this money comes from creditors (liabilities) and how much comes from stockholders (equity). Moreover, the balance sheet gives you an idea of how efficiently your company is utilizing its assets and how well it is managing its liabilities.

Balance sheet data is most helpful when it's compared with information from a previous year. In the table "Amalgamated Hat Rack balance sheet as of December 31, 2008," a comparison of the figures for 2008 against those for 2007 shows that Amalgamated has increased its total liabilities by $38,000 and increased its total assets by $38,000, thus resulting in no change in owners' equity. (Explanations for key terms follow.)

The balance sheet begins by listing the assets that are most easily converted to cash: cash on hand, receivables, and inventory. These are called *current assets*.

Next, the balance sheet tallies other assets that have value but are tougher to convert to cash—for example, buildings and equipment. These are called *fixed or long-term assets*.

Since most long-term assets, except land, depreciate over time, the company must also include accumulated depreciation in this part of the calculation. Gross property, plant, and equipment minus accumulated depreciation equals the current *book value* of property, plant, and equipment.

Tip: The balance sheet distinguishes between short-term liabilities, also known as current liabilities, and long-term liabilities. Short-term liabilities typically have to be paid in a year or less; they include short-term notes, salaries, income taxes, and accounts payable.

Amalgamated Hat Rack balance sheet as of December 31, 2008

	2008	2007	Increase/ (decrease)
Assets			
Cash and marketable securities	$355,000	$430,000	$(75,000)
Accounts receivable	$555,000	$512,000	$43,000
Inventory	$835,000	$755,000	$80,000
Prepaid expenses	$123,000	$98,000	$25,000
Total current assets	**$1,868,000**	**$1,795,000**	**$73,000**
Net property, plant, and equipment	$1,631,000	$1,666,000	$(35,000)
Total assets	**$3,499,000**	**$3,461,000**	**$38,000**
Liabilities and owners' equity			
Accounts payable	$440,000	$430,000	$10,000
Accrued expenses	$98,000	$77,000	$21,000
Income tax payable	$17,000	$9,000	$8,000
Short-term debt	$409,000	$500,000	$(91,000)
Total current liabilities	**$964,000**	**$1,016,000**	**$(52,000)**
Long-term debt	$750,000	$660,000	$90,000
Total liabilities	$1,714,000	$1,676,000	$38,000
Contributed capital	$850,000	$850,000	$0
Retained earnings	$935,000	$935,000	$0
Total owners' equity	**$1,785,000**	**$1,785,000**	**$0**
Total liabilities and owners' equity	**$3,499,000**	**$3,461,000**	**$38,000**

Source: Harvard ManageMentor® on Finance Essentials, adapted with permission.

Subtracting current liabilities from current assets gives you the company's *working capital*. Working capital gives you an idea of how much money the company has tied up in operating activities. Just how much is adequate for the company depends on the industry and the company's plans. For 2008, Amalgamated had $904,000 in working capital.

Most *long-term liabilities* are loans.

Owners' equity comprises *retained earnings* (net profits that accumulate in a company after any dividends are paid) and *contributed capital* (capital received in exchange for stock).

The cash flow statement

A *cash flow statement* gives you a peek into a company's checking account. Like a bank statement, it tells how much cash was on hand at the beginning of the period, and how much was on hand at the end of the period. It then describes how the company spent its cash.

If you're a manager in a large corporation, changes in the company's cash flow won't typically have an impact on your day-to-day functioning. But you can affect cash flow in your company. And it's a good idea to stay up to date with your company's cash flow projections, because they may come into play when you prepare your budget for the upcoming year. For example, if cash is tight, you will probably be asked to be conservative in your spending. Alternatively, if the company is flush with cash, you may have opportunities to make new investments.

If you're a manager in a small company, you're probably keenly aware of the firm's cash flow situation and feel its impact almost every day. The cash flow statement is useful because it shows whether your company is turning profits into cash—and that ability is ultimately what will keep your company solvent. As the example of Amalgamated Hat Rack continues, we see in the table "Amalgamated Hat Rack statement of cash flows, 2008" that the hat rack company generated cash flow of $95,500 in 2008. (Explanations for key terms follow.)

Amalgamated Hat Rack statement of cash flows, 2008

Net income	**$347,500**
Depreciation	$42,500
Accounts receivable	$(43,000)
Inventory	$(80,000)
Prepaid expenses	$(25,000)
Accounts payable	$20,000
Accrued expenses	$21,000
Income tax payable	$8,000
Cash flow from operations	**$291,000**
Property, plant, and equipment (PP&E)	$(7,500)
Cash flow from investing activities	**$(7,500)**
Short-term debt	$(91,000)
Long-term borrowings	$90,000
Contributed capital	$0
Cash dividends to stockholders	$187,000)
Cash flow from financing activities	**$(188,000)**
Increase in cash during year	**$95,500**

Source: Harvard ManageMentor® on Finance Essentials, adapted with permission.

The cash flow statement doesn't measure the same thing as the income statement. If there is no cash transaction, it cannot be reflected on a cash flow statement. Notice, however, that the cash flow statement starts with net income. Then, through a series of adjustments based on the increases and decreases in asset and liability accounts from the balance sheet, the cash flow statement translates this net income to cash.

In general, a company looks to three sources of cash: ongoing operations, investment activities, and financing activities. It's traditional to start with ongoing operations.

ACCOUNTS RECEIVABLE *n* **1.** The amount that customers owe the company for products and services sold but not yet paid for

---

ACCOUNTS PAYABLE *n* **1.** The amount the company owes its vendors for supplies and other items it has received but not yet paid for

---

Investment activities can be:

- Cash the company uses to invest in financial instruments or *property, plant, and equipment* (such investments in PP&E are often shown as *capital expenditures*)
- Proceeds from the sale of plant, property, or equipment
- Proceeds from converting its investments into cash

Financing activities include raising money by borrowing in the capital markets and issuing stock. *Dividends* must be paid out of cash flow; they represent a decrease in cash flow.

Using Financial Statements to Measure Financial Health

THE THREE FINANCIAL statements offer three different perspectives on your company's financial performance. That is, they tell three different but related stories about how well your company is doing financially.

- The *income statement* shows the bottom line: it indicates how much profit or loss a company generates over a period of time—a month, a quarter, or a year.

- The *balance sheet* shows a company's financial position at a specific point in time. That is, it gives a snapshot of the company's financial situation—its assets, liabilities, and equity—on a given day.

- The *cash flow statement* tells where the company's cash comes from and where it goes—in other words, the flow of cash in, through, and out of the company.

Another way to understand the interrelationships is as follows:

- The income statement tells you whether your company is making a profit.

- The balance sheet tells you how efficiently the company is utilizing its assets and how well it is managing its liabilities in pursuit of profits.

- The cash flow statement tells you whether the company is turning profits into cash.

By themselves, financial statements tell you quite a bit: how much profit the company made, where it spent its money, how large its debts are. But how do you *interpret* all the numbers these statements provide? For example, is the company's profit large or small? Is the level of debt healthy or not?

Ratio analysis provides a means of digging deeper into the information contained in the three financial statements. A financial ratio is two key numbers from a company's financial statements expressed in relation to each other. The ratios that follow are relevant across a wide spectrum of industries but are most meaningful when compared against the same measures for other companies in the same industry.

Profitability ratios

These measures evaluate a company's level of profitability by expressing sales and profits as a percentage of various other items.

- *Return on assets (ROA).* ROA provides a quantitative description of how well a company has invested in its assets. To calculate ROA, divide net income by total assets.

- *Return on equity (ROE).* ROE shows the return on the portion of the company's financing that is provided by owners. To calculate ROE, divide net income by owners' equity.

- *Return on sales (ROS).* Also known as net profit margin, ROS is a way to measure how sales translate into bottom-line profit. For example, if a company makes a profit of $10 for every $100 in sales, the ROS is 10/100, or 10 percent. To calculate ROS, divide net income by the revenue.

- *Gross profit margin.* A ratio that measures the percentage of *gross profit* relative to revenue, gross margin reflects the profitability of the company's products or services.

    To calculate gross margin, divide gross profit by revenue.

- *Earnings before interest and taxes (EBIT) margin.* Many analysts use this indicator, also known as *operating margin*, to see how profitable a company's operating activities are.

    To calculate EBIT margin, divide operating profit by revenue.

Operating ratios

By linking various income statement and balance sheet figures, these measures provide an assessment of a company's operating efficiency.

- *Asset turnover.* This shows how efficiently a company uses its assets.

Tip: To calculate asset turnover, divide revenue by total assets. The higher the number, the better.

- *Days receivables.* It's best to collect on receivables promptly. This measure tells you in concrete terms how long it actually takes a company to collect what it's owed. A company that takes forty-five days to collect its receivables will need significantly more working capital than one that takes four days to collect.

There are different methods to calculate days receivables. One way is to divide ending accounts receivable by revenue per day.

- *Days payables.* This measure tells you how many days it takes a company to pay its suppliers. The more days it takes, the longer a company has the cash to work with.

  There are different methods to calculate days payables. One way is to divide ending accounts payable by cost of goods sold per day.

- *Days inventory.* This is a measure of how long it takes a company to sell the average amount of inventory on hand during a given period of time. The longer it takes to sell the inventory, the more the company's cash gets tied up and the greater the likelihood that the inventory will not be sold at full value.

  To calculate days inventory, divide average inventory by cost of goods sold per day.

Liquidity ratios

Liquidity ratios tell you about a company's ability to meet its financial obligations, including debt, payroll, vendor payments, and so on.

- *Current ratio.* This is a prime measure of how solvent a company is. It's so popular with lenders that it's sometimes called the *banker's ratio.* Generally speaking, the higher the ratio, the better financial condition a company is in. A company that has $3.2 million in current assets and $1.2 million in current liabilities would have a current ratio of 2.7 to 1. That company would be generally healthier than one with a current ratio of 2.2 to 1.

To calculate the current ratio, divide total current assets by total current liabilities.

- *Quick ratio.* This ratio isn't faster to compute than any other—it simply measures the ratio of a company's assets that can be quickly liquidated and used to pay debts. Thus, it ignores inventory, which can be hard to liquidate (and if you do have to liquidate inventory quickly, you typically get less for it than you would otherwise). This ratio is sometimes called the *acid-test ratio* because it measures a company's ability to deal instantly with its liabilities.

  To calculate the quick ratio, divide current assets minus inventory by current liabilities.

Leverage ratios

Leverage ratios tell you how, and how extensively, a company uses debt. In the world of finance, the word *leverage* is used for debt.

- *Interest coverage.* This measures a company's margin of safety: how many times over the company can make its interest payments.

  To calculate interest coverage, divide income before interest and taxes by interest expense.

- **Debt to equity.** This measure provides a description of how well the company is making use of borrowed money to enhance the return on owners' equity.

  To calculate the debt-to-equity ratio, divide total liabilities by owners' equity.

Other ways to measure financial health

Beyond profitability, operating, and leverage ratios, other ways of evaluating the financial health of a company include valuation, Economic Value Added (EVA), and assessing growth and productivity. Like the ratios described above, all these measures are most meaningful when compared against the same measures for other companies in that particular industry.

Valuation. Valuation often refers to the process by which people determine the total value of a company for the purpose of selling it. This type of valuation is an uncertain science. For example, a firm that is considering acquiring another firm might rely heavily on estimates of future cash flows to come up with a value for the potential acquisition. Another firm might rely on different data. Also, a company is worth different amounts to different parties. For instance, a small, high-tech company may be valued more by a potential acquirer that wants the acquired firm's unique technology to leverage its other operations.

Valuation also refers to the process that Wall Street investors and stock analysts use to scrutinize a company's financial statements and stock performance carefully in order to arrive at what they believe to be a realistic estimate of that company's value. Since a share of stock denotes ownership of a part of the company, analysts are interested in knowing whether the market price of that share is a good deal, relative to the underlying value of the piece of the company the share represents.

Wall Street uses various means of valuation—that is, of assessing a company's financial performance in relation to its stock price.

- The *earnings per share (EPS)* equals net income divided by the number of shares outstanding. This is one of the most commonly watched indicators of a company's financial performance. If it falls, it will likely take the stock's price down with it.

- The *price-to-earnings ratio (P/E)* is the current price of a share of stock divided by the previous twelve months' earnings per share. It is a common measure of how cheap or expensive a stock is, relative to earnings.

- *Growth indicators.* Growth measures can tell a great deal about financial health. A company's *growth* allows it to provide increasing returns to its shareholders and to provide opportunities for new and existing employees. The number of years over which you should measure growth will depend on the business cycle of the industry the company is in. A one-year growth figure for an oil company—an industry that typically has long business cycles—probably doesn't tell you very much. But a strong one-year growth figure for an

Internet company would be significant. Common measures of growth include sales growth, profitability growth, and growth in earnings per share.

Economic Value Added. This concept was introduced as a way to induce employees to think like shareholders and owners. It is the profit left over after the company has met the expectations of those who provided the capital.

Productivity measures. Sales-per-employee and net-income-per-employee measures link revenue and profit generation information to workforce data. Watching the trends of these numbers adds to your understanding of what is occurring in the company.

Tips: Analyzing Financial Statements

- Consider the context—what looks like a big (or small) number may not be once you understand what's typical for a business in that particular industry.
- Compare one company's statements with those of a similar-sized company within the same industry.
- Watch for trends. How have the statements changed since last year? From three years ago?
- Use your company's statements to write a paragraph that describes how much profit it is making, how well it is managing its assets, where the money comes from, and where it goes.

The Budget Process

A BUDGET IS A blueprint for achieving specific goals. Your unit's budget is part of your company's overall strategy. So you need to understand your company's strategy in order to create a useful budget.

How can you familiarize yourself with your company's overall strategy?

- **Watch the overall economic picture.** A company's strategy during a recession will be far different than in a booming economy. Make a point to listen to your manager's and colleagues' views on sales and the economy—and make your own observations as well. Are you deluged by résumés, or is good help hard to find? Are prices rising or falling?

- **Stay on top of industry trends.** Even when the economy is booming, some sectors are going bust; your budget will need to reflect that reality.

- **Steep yourself in company values.** Every company has values, sometimes formalized and sometimes just "the way we do things." The very best companies keep those values in mind during every decision. Suppose your budget calls for a cut in the company's contribution to health-care plans. If the company's values view such cuts as anathema to its overall commitment to employees, your proposal will be dead on arrival.

- Conduct *SWOT analyses*. Every company has strengths, weaknesses, opportunities, and threats. Keep them in mind as you build your budget.

Understanding top-down and bottom-up budgeting

If your company does top-down budgeting, senior management sets very specific objectives for such things as net income, profit margins, and expenses. For instance, each department may be told to hold expense increases to no more than 6 percent above last year's levels. It's left up to you to allocate your budget within the parameters to ensure that the objectives are achieved. For example, suppose Amalgamated Hat Rack decides that it wants to increase overall profitability by 10 percent. That could mean, among other possibilities, launching a new product line to generate new sales, or cutting overhead by upgrading technology, which would reduce the need for part-time workers.

In addition, if your company does top-down budgeting, make sure to look at the overall plans for sales and marketing, as well as cost and expense plans, as you prepare your budget. The company's sales plan determines, to a large extent, how much money will be available for the budget. The marketing budget will give you an idea of what the company will be emphasizing in the coming year. Further, many companies strive to reduce expenses as a percentage of revenue every year, no matter how slightly, as a way to improve profitability.

In companies that do bottom-up budgeting, managers aren't given specific targets. Instead, they begin by putting together budgets

What Would YOU Do?

Was the Budget on Track?

S IMONE WAS PLEASED. Recently promoted as manager of her company's human resource department, she had worked hard to develop the budget for her unit for the coming year. She had negotiated with management for the resources she needed, had made the assumptions behind her requests crystal clear, and had checked to be certain that her budget aligned with the company's strategy. But Simone also knew that preparing her budget and getting it approved were just the beginning steps in the budgeting process. As the coming year unfolded, she would have to find ways to assess whether the budget she had worked so hard to create was staying on track—or going off the rails. Though she understood the importance of tracking her budget, she felt somewhat uncertain about how to approach this responsibility.

that they feel will best meet the needs and goals of their respective departments. These budgets are then "rolled up" to create an overall company budget, which is then adjusted, with requests for changes being sent back down to the individual departments.

This process can go through multiple iterations. Often it means working closely with other departments that may be competing against yours for limited resources. It's best to be as cooperative as you can with other departments during this process, but that doesn't mean you shouldn't lobby aggressively for your own unit's needs.

Preparing a budget

As a manager, you are expected to put together a budget for your department each year. Your compensation may depend, to a large extent, on your ability to stick to that budget. So it's in your best interest to create a realistic budget when you start out. But don't sandbag either; it won't do you or your company any good.

Begin by setting goals. You may want to improve your division's performance over the previous year, increase net income for the company, or decrease costs—maybe even all three. How do you think your department can accomplish everything it has set out to do? That's where the budget comes into play. After all, a budget is a plan with numbers.

Start with a list of three to five goals that you'd like to achieve—and put a completion date on them, too. For example:

- Increase gross sales by 5 percent by June 30.

- Decrease administrative costs by 3 percent as a percentage of revenue by the end of the fiscal year.

- Reduce inventories by 2 percent by the end of the fiscal year.

Be sure you know the scope of the budget you're supposed to produce. Scope implies two things: the part of the company the budget is supposed to cover and the level of detail it should include.

- The smaller the unit that you're focusing on, the more you need to budget at the detail level. If you're creating a budget for a twelve-person sales office, you typically won't need to worry about such capital expenditures as major upgrades to the building or the computer equipment. But you should include estimates of what kinds of office supplies you'll need and how much they will cost.

- As you move up the organizational ladder to include more people and larger departments in your budgeting, your scope broadens. You can assume that the head of the twelve-person office has thought about paper clips and travel expenses. You're now looking at capital expenditures, studying the broad-brush outline and looking at how it all rolls up together.

Other issues to consider:

- **Term.** Is the budget just for this year, or the next five years? Most budgets are for the upcoming year, with quarterly or monthly reviews.

- **Overview.** Does your budget need to be accompanied by an overview of your strategic plan—for example, your plans for increasing sales or market share? If so, you need to be prepared to defend it.

Take a hard look at your assumptions for the coming year. After all, a budget, at its simplest, takes current data, adds assumptions,

Steps for Creating a Budget

1. Analyze your company's overall strategy.
2. If your company does top-down budgeting, start with the targets given to you by senior management. If your company does bottom-up budgeting, create these targets yourself.
3. Articulate your assumptions.
4. Quantify your assumptions.
5. Review: Do the numbers add up? Can you document your assumptions? Is your budget defensible?

and creates projections. Let's suppose you think sales will rise 10 percent in the coming year. If that's true, you may have to add two more people to your unit. But when you get before your budget committee, be prepared to defend your assumption that sales will rise 10 percent.

Role-playing may help you here. Put yourself in the position of a division manager with limited resources and many departmental requests for funding. How can you make your case for two additional staff members so that the division manager grants your request ahead of all the others?

Articulating your assumptions

The easiest way to get started is to take a look at your department's most recent budget. If you're the manager of Amalgamated Hat

Rack's Moose Head Division, you might decide to look at the 2009 budget (shown in the table "Moose Head Division, Amalgamated Hat Rack") to get ideas about how to increase revenues, cut costs—or both.

Moose Head Division, Amalgamated Hat Rack

2009 Budget	Budgeted	Actual	Variance
Sales by model			
Moose Antler Deluxe	$237,000	$208,560	$(28,440)
Moose Antler Standard	$320,225	$329,832	$9,607
Standard Upright	$437,525	$476,902	$39,377
Electro-Revolving	$125,000	$81,250	$(43,750)
Hall/Wall	$80,000	$70,400	$(9,600)
Total sales	**$1,199,750**	**$1,166,944**	**$(32,806)**
Cost of goods sold			
Direct labor	$75,925	$82,000	$(6,075)
Factory overhead	$5,694	$6,150	$(456)
Direct materials	$195,000	$191,100	$3,900
Total cost of goods sold	**$276,619**	**$279,250**	**$(2,631)**
Sales, general, and administrative costs			
Sales salaries	$300,000	$310,000	$(10,000)
Advertising expenses	$135,000	$140,000	$(5,000)
Miscellaneous selling expenses	$3,400	$2,500	$900
Office expenses	$88,000	$90,000	$(2,000)
Total SG&A	**$526,400**	**$542,500**	**$(16,100)**
Operating income	**$396,731**	**$345,194**	**$(51,537)**

Source: Harvard ManageMentor® on Finance Essentials, adapted with permission.

Don't start off by looking at specific revenue or cost line items, because revenues and costs are integrally linked. Instead, begin by asking yourself what events you want to see happen over the time frame you'll be budgeting for and what revenues and expenses are associated with each.

For example, do you expect to sell more products? How? If you plan to increase sales of your company's current products, there will be additional sales and marketing costs—maybe even new hires—associated with this strategy. Or if you intend to expand the company's product line, you will need to budget for a new product development initiative.

In the case of the Moose Head Division, the Standard Upright and Moose Antler Standard exceeded sales expectations in 2009. If these have the highest sales numbers, would it make sense to increase the sales projections for them, or should you stick with the 2009 sales volume for your 2010 projection? If you're looking to increase sales volume, the Standard Upright is a good choice: it beat its 2009 projection by 9 percent. Could you increase the anticipated sales for this model by 5 percent or 10 percent in 2010? In order to achieve this increase, how much more would you need to spend on marketing? To make the decisions, you'll also need pricing, market, and other relevant data.

Alternatively, do you expect to eliminate some products? At Amalgamated, the Electro-Revolving model is faring poorly. Would it be better to eliminate this line entirely and promote the newer Hall/Wall model? It would eliminate $81,250 in sales, but since the Electro-Revolving is very expensive to produce, perhaps the net result of discontinuation would not affect the bottom line very much.

Other questions to ask yourself include:

- Will you keep prices the same, lower them, or raise them? A price increase of 3 percent would have more than eliminated the budget's 2009 gross sales shortfall—provided that the increase did not dampen sales.

- Do you plan to enter new markets, target new customers, or use new sales strategies? How much additional revenue do you expect these efforts to bring in? How much will these initiatives cost?

- Will your salary expenses change? For example, do you plan to cut down on temporary help and replace these resources with full-time employees? Or will you be able to reduce salary costs through automation? If so, how much will it cost to automate?

- Are your suppliers likely to raise or lower prices? Are you planning to switch to lower-cost suppliers? Will there be a drop-off in quality? If so, how much will it affect your sales?

- Will your product have to be enhanced to keep your current customers?

- Do you need to train your staff?

- Are there other special projects or initiatives you are planning to pursue?

Quantifying your assumptions

Each of your assumptions and scenarios must be translated into dollar figures. If your entire staff of twelve needs sales training, you need to find out how much it will cost to train each person, and multiply that number by twelve to calculate the total cost. Some costs or revenues are easier to project than others—which is why it's always a good idea not to prepare your budget alone. Coworkers and direct reports will have valuable suggestions. Trade publications can often provide industry averages for a range of costs.

Once you've translated the assumptions into numbers, you need to incorporate those numbers into budget line items. Because your budget needs to be compared and combined with others, your company will probably provide you with a standard set of line items to use. In some cases, your quantified assumptions will constitute the entire line item —for example, you may have listed and quantified all the product development projects you'll be pursuing next year. In other cases, your assumptions will be incremental: if you plan to boost sales by raising prices, you'll start with last year's sales figures and then increase them by the appropriate amount.

Tip: As you put your budget into its required format, be sure to document your assumptions. It's easy to lose track during the translation, and you will want to be able to explain them—and revise them—when needed.

When you have compiled your budget, take a step back. Does the budget meet the goals that have been set for your unit? For example, if your goal was to increase gross sales by 5 percent, does the budget in fact do so? It's easy to overlook overall goals as you get into the line-by-line detail.

Furthermore, is your budget defensible? You may be perfectly happy with it, but not everyone else on the budget committee may be. Once again, you have to push your assumptions. Could you do as well with one extra staff member as with two? If not, be sure you can prove it.

Tips: Budgeting

- **Stay goal oriented.** If you aim to increase sales, make that the overriding concern of your budget. Don't let other issues sidetrack you from your main goal.
- **Be realistic.** Most new managers would like to double sales or cut expenses in half. But remember: you'll be held accountable for the results.
- **Don't try to do it alone.** Include your team members—they may have detailed knowledge about certain line items that you don't.
- **Don't use the budget as a substitute for regular communication with your staff.** Team members should hear directly from you about the funding for line items that affect them most directly— not by reading the finalized budget.
- **Don't blame denied requests on the budget.** Be direct: tell an employee if a requested business trip is unlikely to be worth the expense, instead of saying, "We just don't have money in the budget."

?

What You COULD Do.

Remember Simone and her need to track her budget for the HR department?

Simone needs to assess the performance of her budget at least monthly. In particular, she should pay special attention to large positive and negative variances, and figure out what's causing them. For example, a variance might be a one-time variation—in which case Simone wouldn't need to change anything. Still, she should keep monitoring such variances over subsequent months to make sure they do indeed straighten themselves out. If a variance *doesn't* represent a one-time aberration, Simone will need to assess why the variances are occurring and develop responses to them—which she could do by brainstorming ideas with her team.

In addition to tracking and addressing variances, she should also reassess forecasts quarterly as well as inform senior management if it looks as if she's not going to make her annual budget goals. That way, management can adjust the overall company forecast accordingly. Finally, Simone should also inform senior management if her unit's performance is turning out *better* than expected. And by saving her original budget assumptions and estimates, she'll be able to improve her budgeting ability for next year.

What Is Cost/Benefit Analysis?

*The safest way to double
your money is to fold it over once
and put it in your pocket.*
—Frank McKinney Hubbard

AMALGAMATED RAT HACK is considering two investment options: buying a new piece of machinery and creating a new product line. The new machine is a plastic extruder
costing $100,000. Amalgamated hopes it will save time and money
over the long term, in addition to being safer than the current machinery. The second option, launching a line of coatracks, will require a $250,000 investment in plant, equipment, and design.

How does Amalgamated decide whether these investment options make economic sense?

The process of determining the answer is known as *cost/benefit
analysis*. Basically, this means evaluating whether, over a given
time frame, the benefits of the new investment or the new business
opportunity outweigh the associated costs.

Before you begin any cost/benefit analysis, it's important to understand the cost of the status quo. You want to weigh the relative
merits of each investment against the negative consequences, if
any, of not proceeding with the investment. Don't assume that the
costs of doing nothing are always high: in many cases, even when

significant benefits could be gained from a new investment, the cost of doing nothing is relatively low. (See the "Initiative Proposal Worksheet" in the Tips and Tools section.)

Steps of cost/benefit analysis

The cost/benefit analysis of a particular investment involves the following steps:

1. Identify all the costs of the new purchase or business opportunity.

2. Identify the benefits of additional revenues.

3. Identify the cost savings to be gained.

4. Map out the timeline for expected costs and anticipated revenues.

5. Evaluate the unquantifiable benefits and costs.

The first three steps are fairly straightforward. First, begin by identifying all the costs associated with the venture—this year's up-front costs as well as the ones you anticipate in subsequent years. Second, determine additional revenue that could come from more customers or from increased purchases from existing customers. To understand the benefits of these revenues, make sure to factor in the new expenses associated with them; ultimately, this means you'll be looking at profit. Third, cost savings can arise

What Would YOU Do?

The Case of the Frustrated Fortune-Teller

FRANÇOIS REALIZED MONTHS ago that his company needed to make significant inroads into the young-adult market. He made numerous presentations to senior management on new product concepts, market studies, and extensive competitive analysis. At the end of each presentation, he cautioned that if the company didn't move into this market soon, its competitors would beat the company to it. Finally, senior management said, "We need to understand the bottom line. Give us some projections." Projections? How could he confidently predict how much money the company would make at some future date? He wasn't a fortune-teller.

from a variety of sources; for the ones listed below, it isn't hard to quantify the savings.

- **More efficient processing.** This could mean that fewer people are required to do the processing, or that the process requires fewer steps, or even that the time spent on each step decreases.

- **More accurate processing.** The time required to correct errors and the number of lost customers could both decrease.

But be sure not to double-count cost savings in your expenses that go along with your additional revenue. Many times, the investment will either increase revenue or decrease expenses, but not both. So you'll do *either* step 2 *or* step 3.

In step 4, map out these two elements—the costs and the revenues or cost savings—over the relevant period of time. When do you expect the costs to be incurred? In what increments? When do you expect to receive the benefits (additional revenues or cost savings)? In what increments?

Once that's done, you're ready to begin the evaluation phase, using one or more of the following analytical tools:

- Net return (sometimes referred to as ROI)

- Payback period

- Breakeven analysis

- Net present value (NPV)

- Sensitivity analysis

Let's take a closer look at each of these tools.

Net return and payback period

Net return (sometimes called return on investment, or ROI) describes financial analysis of capital expenditures. To calculate net return, first subtract the total cost of the investment from the total benefits of the return. Then divide the net dollar amount of return by the total cost of the investment. This can help you compare returns on money your company spends internally with returns available elsewhere. However, because it does not address what is called the time value of money (to be addressed shortly), it does not provide the full picture.

Let's suppose that the new $100,000 plastic extruder Amalgamated is considering would enable the company to save $18,000 a year over the lifetime of the machine, which would be seven years. The total savings would thus be $126,000, making for a net dollar return of $26,000. Applying the formula—$26,000 divided by $100,000—the net return for the investment is a very attractive 26 percent.

But companies also want to know the *payback period*: how long it will take a particular investment to pay for itself. We already know that the plastic extruder is expected to save Amalgamated $18,000 a year. To determine the payback period, divide the total amount of the investment by the annual savings expected. In this case, $100,000 divided by $18,000 equals 5.56. In other words, the extruder will pay for itself in 5.56 years. The table "Amalgamated extruder savings" provides a year-by-year illustration.

Note that Amalgamated will not truly begin to reap the benefits of the investment for more than five years.

As analytical tools, net return and payback period have several benefits:

- They're easy to convey to upper management.
- They remind everyone that wise expenditures pay off financially.
- They adopt a long-term perspective.
- They help you compare different options.

Amalgamated extruder savings		
Year	**Savings**	**Cumulative savings**
1	$18,000	$18,000
2	$18,000	$36,000
3	$18,000	$54,000
4	$18,000	$72,000
5	$18,000	$90,000
6	$18,000	$108,000
7	$18,000	$126,000

Source: Harvard ManageMentor® on Finance Essentials, adapted with permission.

There is a drawback to both methods, however: they do not provide as accurate an economic picture as more sophisticated tools such as net present value and internal rate of return, because they ignore the time value of money.

Net present value and internal rate of return

These two analytical tools can be fairly complicated. Because most calculators and spreadsheet programs can make these calculations for you, we're only going to describe them broadly.

To begin, consider the principle that underlies both methods: the *time value of money*. In effect, this principle states that a dollar you receive today is worth more than a dollar you receive five years from today. The reason: even assuming no inflation, the dollar you receive today can be invested somewhere, which means that you will have more than a dollar by the fifth year.

Evaluating a new business opportunity means analyzing the income you expect that opportunity to provide at some point in the future. To perform that analysis, you'll be using a method for expressing future dollars in terms of current dollars. That's what *net present value* (NPV) and *internal rate of return* (IRR) calculations allow you to do.

Let's say that Amalgamated expects its new product line to start generating a cash flow of $60,000 annually, beginning one year from now and continuing for the succeeding five years. The questions for the company can thus be phrased as follows: given this expected cash flow stream and the $250,000 up-front cost required to produce it, is a new line of coatracks the most productive way to invest that initial $250,000? Or would Amalgamated be better off investing it in something else?

A net present value calculation begins answering these questions by recognizing that the $300,000 in cash flow that Amalgamated expects to receive over five years is not worth $300,000 in current dollars. Because of the time value of money, it is worth less than that. In other words, that future sum of $300,000 has to be *discounted* in order to be expressed accurately in today's dollars. *How much* it is discounted depends on the rate of return Amalgamated could reasonably expect to receive had it chosen to put the initial $250,000 investment into something other than the line of coatracks (but similar in risk) for the same period of time. This rate of return is often called the discount rate. In the Amalgamated example, assume a discount rate of 6 percent. The NPV function on your calculator or spreadsheet takes into consideration your initial investment, your yearly cash flow, your discount rate, and the time period (in years) that you are analyzing.

An NPV calculation determines the net present value of a series of cash flows according to the following algebraic formula:

$$\text{Net Present Value} = \text{Cash Flow } (CF)_0 + \frac{CF_1}{(1+i)^1} + \frac{CF_2}{(1+i)^2} + \frac{CF_n}{(1+i)^n}$$

where each CF is a future cash flow, n is the number of years over which the cash flow stream is expected to occur, and i is the desired rate of return, or the discount rate.

When you supply the values for each future cash flow, the discount rate, and the number of years, your spreadsheet or calculator will do the rest.

If the resulting NPV is a positive number, and no other investments are under consideration, the investment should be pursued. In the Amalgamated case, the NPV for the line of coatracks is $2,587, which suggests that it would be an attractive investment for Amalgamated. (Note: if the initial investment is made at the *end* of the first period, the NPV is $2,587. If the initial investment is made at the *beginning* of the first period, the NPV is $2,742. For the purposes of this example, we will use $2,587 as the NPV.)

But what about the other investment Amalgamated is considering, the $100,000 plastic extruder? At a discount rate of 6 percent, the NPV is $456, which is just barely positive. When we compare NPVs for the two investments—remember that the discount rate for each scenario is 6 percent—we see that both are positive, but the one for the coatracks is more positive. If Amalgamated could afford only one of these investments, therefore, it should go with the new line of coatracks.

Here, the effect that the discount rate has on the NPV should be emphasized. Suppose the discount rate were 10 percent instead of

6 percent: in that case, the NPV for the extruder would be $-11,244. The extruder would go from being a modestly attractive investment to being a very poor one.

Notice something else about the NPV calculation for the extruder: even with a 6 percent discount rate, the NPV is far less optimistic than the rosy 26 percent net return forecast. The point here is that although it's much more difficult to perform—and explain—the NPV analysis does result in more sophisticated, more comprehensive evaluations of investment opportunities.

Typically, when the *internal rate of return* is greater than the opportunity cost (the expected return on a comparable investment) of the capital required, the investment under consideration should be undertaken.

INTERNAL RATE OF RETURN (IRR) *n* **1.** A means for managers to decide whether to commit to a particular investment opportunity. IRR is the actual return provided by the projected cash flows. That rate of return can then be compared with the company's *hurdle rate*—the minimum rate of return that all investments for a particular enterprise must achieve.

The IRR calculation is based on the same algebraic formula as the NPV calculation. With the NPV calculation, you know the desired rate of return and are solving the equation for the net present value of the future cash flows. With IRR, by contrast, the net present value is set at zero, and the equation is solved for the rate of return. Your spreadsheet program or calculator will perform IRR calculations for you, just as it will for NPV.

What's a reasonable rate of return for a business to expect on an investment comparable to the one under consideration? Typically, it's well above what it could get on a risk-free investment, such as a Treasury bond. In many instances, companies will set a *hurdle rate*, a minimum rate of return that all investments are required to achieve. In such instances, the IRR of the investment under consideration must exceed the hurdle rate in order for the company to go forward with it.

If we return to Amalgamated's coatrack opportunity, the calculation yields an IRR for this investment of 6.4 percent, which is slightly above the discount rate of 6 percent. If Amalgamated's hurdle rate were 6 percent, it would go ahead with the new line of coatracks. But if the hurdle rate were 10 percent, the 6.4 percent IRR would mean that Amalgamated should not make the investment.

Breakeven analysis

Breakeven analysis is useful when considering an investment that will enable you to sell something new or to sell more of something you already make. It tells you how much (or how much more) you need to sell in order to pay for the fixed investment—in other words, at what point you will break even. With that information in hand, you can look at market demand and competitors' market shares to determine whether it's realistic to expect to sell that much. (See the "Breakeven Analysis Worksheet" in the Tools and Resources section.)

In more precise terms, the breakeven calculation helps you determine the volume level at which total contribution from a product line or an investment equals total fixed costs. But before you can perform the calculation, you need to understand the components that go into it.

- **Contribution** is defined as unit revenue minus variable costs per unit; it's the money available to contribute to paying fixed costs.

- **Fixed costs** are items such as insurance, management salaries, rent, and product development costs—they're items that stay pretty much the same no matter how many units of a product or service are sold.

- **Variable costs** are those expenses that change depending on how many units are produced and sold; examples would include labor, utility costs, and raw materials.

With these concepts, you can understand the calculation:

- Subtract the variable cost per unit from the unit revenue—this is the unit contribution.

- Divide total fixed costs, or the amount of the investment, by the unit contribution.

- The quotient is the breakeven volume, expressed as the number of units that must be sold in order for all fixed costs to be covered.

Consider the example of the new line of coatracks again. Suppose the new coatracks sell for $75, and the variable cost per unit is $22. The table "Breakeven calculation" shows how to determine the breakeven volume for the coatracks.

Breakeven calculation

$75 (unit revenue)
− 22 (variable cost per unit)
$53 (unit contribution)

$250,000 (total investment required)
÷ 53 (unit contribution)
4,717 coatracks (breakeven volume)

Source: Harvard ManageMentor® on Finance Essentials, adapted with permission.

At this point, Amalgamated must decide whether the breakeven volume is achievable: is it realistic to expect to sell 4,717 additional coatracks, and if so, how quickly? To calculate the breakeven volume for the extruder, you would define the unit contribution as the cost savings per unit.

Sensitivity analysis

As noted earlier, Amalgamated would expect its new line of coatracks to begin generating $60,000 in annual profit beginning a year from now. But what if some variable in the scenario changed—how would it affect the overall evaluation of the investment opportunity? Sensitivity analysis enables you to ask just this kind of question and to see the ramifications of incremental changes in the assumptions that underlie a particular projection.

Sherman Peaboddy is the vice president of Amalgamated's Moose Head Division. He would exercise day-to-day oversight of the new product line, and he is the one projecting $60,000 in annual profit for five years. Natasha Rubskaya, the company's CFO, is more phlegmatic about the investment, primarily because she believes that Peaboddy has drastically underestimated the marketing costs necessary to support the new line. She predicts an annual profit stream of $45,000. Then there's Theodore Bullmoose, Amalgamated's senior vice president for new business development. Ever the optimist, he is convinced that the coatracks will practically sell themselves, producing an annual profit stream of $75,000 a year.

Amalgamated conducts a sensitivity analysis using the three different profit scenarios. The NPV for Peaboddy's is $2,587. For Rubskaya's, it's $–57,022. And for Bullmoose's scenario, the NPV is $62,196.

If Rubskaya is right, the coatracks won't be worth the investment. If either of the other two is right, however, the investment will be worthwhile—marginally so, according to Peaboddy's profit projections, and very much so, according to Bullmoose's. This is where judgment comes into play. If Natasha Rubskaya is the best estimator of the three, Amalgamated's board of directors might prefer to take her estimate of the coatrack line's profit potential. Better still, the company should analyze its marketing costs in greater detail.

Whichever route they take, the sensitivity analysis will give the board of directors a more nuanced view of the investment and how it would be affected by various changes in assumptions. Other contingencies, or changes in other variables, could be mapped out just as easily.

Estimating unquantifiable benefits and costs

The numbers don't tell the whole story, so your cost/benefit analysis should incorporate qualitative factors as well. Examples here include the strategic fit of the new opportunity with the company's mission, the ability to take on the new opportunity without losing focus, the likelihood of success given market conditions, and perhaps an increase in customer goodwill that the new investment would bring about.

- **Even though such factors are not fully quantifiable, try to quantify them as much as possible.** Make assumptions that can help you come up with a ballpark figure. Suppose you're trying to assess the value of improved information—more comprehensive data that is easier to understand and more widely available—that a new investment would bring. You could try to come up with a dollar figure that represents the value of employees' time saved by the new information or the value of the increased customer retention that might be gleaned from better understanding purchase patterns. Such estimates should not necessarily be incorporated into your ROI or NPV analysis, but they can be very persuasive nevertheless.

- **Weigh the quantifiable and the unquantifiable factors.** For example, if the net present value of an investment opportunity is only marginally positive, you may want to give more qualitative considerations, such as strategic fit, an equal weight in your final decision.

What You COULD Do.

> Let's go back to François's problem of coming up with projections for making inroads into the young-adult market.

François might begin by performing a cost/benefit analysis on a particular product he has in mind for serving the young-adult market. A cost/benefit analysis identifies, over a given time frame, the costs and benefits of developing the product and then compares those figures to see whether launching the product makes economic sense. Once François has performed the cost/benefit analysis, he can further evaluate the proposed product's potential by using one or more of the following analytical tools: net return, payback period, breakeven analysis, net present value, and sensitivity analysis.

The information, or projections, that François gathers will help senior management understand the bottom line of the proposed product and determine whether the company should invest in it. For example, if François's various analyses indicate that the return on investing in the product doesn't meet his company's hurdle rate, then the firm may decide not to develop the product.

Tracking Performance

REGARDLESS OF WHETHER you're tracking an investment opportunity you've decided to undertake or the annual budget you've created for your unit, you need to monitor your ongoing results to make sure your projections are on course. Just how closely you should keep tabs on the results depends on your level of management. If you're an office manager, you should be aware of how much you're spending on paper clips and travel costs; if you're a division manager, your focus is probably at a bigger-picture level.

Tracking the performance of an investment

When you evaluate a new investment, you're planning for the long term—typically a year or more. But in the real world, things change and plans go awry. And estimates are valid only for a limited period of time. Your first task, therefore, is to track your projections versus actual revenues and expenses. It's a good idea to do this on a monthly basis so that you can spot potential problems early on.

Consider the projections for the new Coatrack Division at Amalgamated Hat Rack. Management ended up using Theodore Bullmoose's optimistic profit projections. The table "Amalgamated Hat Rack, Coatrack Division, January 2011 results" shows the state of affairs early in the first quarter.

Amalgamated Hat Rack, Coatrack Division, January 2011 results

Item	Budget Jan.	Actual Jan.	Variance
Coatrack revenues	$39,000	$38,725	$(275)
Cost of goods sold	$19,500	$19,200	$(300)
Gross margin	$19,500	$19,525	$25
Marketing	$8,500	$10,100	$(1,600)
Administrative expense	$4,750	$4,320	$430
Total operating expense	$13,250	$14,420	$(1,170)
Operating profit	**$6,250**	**$5,105**	**$(1,145)**

Source: Harvard ManageMentor® on Finance Essentials, adapted with permission.

The division is doing reasonably well on revenues and cost of goods sold. Its only really large negative variance is in the marketing expense line. It's difficult to be certain based on just the first month's figures: is this simply a one-time, or seasonal, variation, or is Amalgamated going to have to spend more on marketing than Bullmoose had anticipated?

If your investment is not tracking according to budget, and if it looks as if the pattern of unexpectedly high costs (or unexpectedly low revenues) is going to hold, it may be necessary to rethink the initiative—or even to discontinue it. In the coatrack example, Amalgamated decides, after further investigation, that the higher-than-expected marketing costs will continue—and Bullmoose's prediction that the coatracks would sell themselves will not be borne out. The revised forecast, however, confirms Sherman Peaboddy's forecast about marketing costs and an annual profit stream of $60,000. The new line of coatracks still seems to be economically viable but not the huge success that Bullmoose believed it would be.

Tracking your budget

Tracking the budget for an already established unit involves many of the same procedures discussed above, but the continue-discontinue decision doesn't come into play as readily. Instead, managers monitor results in order to be able to make necessary spending or operating adjustments as quickly as possible. (See the "Annual Budgeting and Tracking Worksheet" in the Tools and Resources section.)

For line items that contain surprises, ask first whether the reason has to do with timing. In other words, do you have a monthly aberration or a long-term problem? If you suspect an aberration, you don't need to be too concerned—the situation should straighten itself out. Nevertheless, be sure to keep a close eye on those particular line items during subsequent months.

If the cause of the variance is not an aberration, however, you need to determine why the variances occurred. Then you should

---

Steps for Tracking Performance of an Investment

1. Assess monthly revenue performance versus budget.
2. Assess monthly expense performance versus budget.
3. Determine whether—and if so, how—your bottom line will be affected by any variances.

---

decide how you should respond as well as revise your forecasts, if necessary. Try to uncover what other reasons may lie beneath your faulty projections. Maybe expenses are higher than budgeted because sales have increased sharply—in which case, expense overruns would be good news rather than bad. In many cases, however, you'll have to try to find some way to make up the loss. Can you decrease spending for certain line items—to compensate for line items that are over budget?

Tip: Make sure to involve team members in figuring out how to address variances.

If it doesn't look as if you're going to make your budget, communicate this to upper management. That way, it can make appropriate adjustments in the overall company forecast. It may also provide you with direction on whether and how to address the shortfalls.

And last, reassess your forecasts quarterly. Budgets are made annually, but estimates are often inaccurate. It's not unusual to miss on your estimates from time to time. Reassessing quarterly is a good way to check your forecasts against reality. Updating your forecasts regularly ensures that you and senior management always have the latest and most accurate information to base decisions on.

But when you do adjust your forecasts, don't throw out the old estimates. When budget time rolls around next year, you'll want to be able to assess how accurate your original assumptions were. This will help you improve your estimates the next time around.

Financial Plan

THE FINANCIAL PLAN is a critical section of any business plan because it translates all the other parts of the business—the opportunity, the operating plan, the marketing plan, the management team—into anticipated financial results. To prepare a financial plan, start by thinking about your readers' concerns.

Anticipating readers' concerns

Different readers of your business plan will have different points of view as they approach the financial plan:

- The *investment committee member* reviewing your proposal wants to know whether the venture can achieve the company's hurdle rate (the minimum rate of return expected of all projects).

- The *investor* considering buying into the venture, whether an outside investor or your department's VP, wants to know what kind of return on investment the business will achieve.

- The *lender* deciding whether to approve a loan wants to know about the borrowing capacity of the company, its ability to service debt.

- Perhaps most important, *you* need to know whether your financial objectives will be achieved—whether all your planning and efforts are going to pay off in the end.

This section of your business plan is where you show your readers the current status and future projections of the initiative's financial performance. The financial picture you paint here represents your best estimate of the risks involved and the return on investment, the tangible evidence of commercial success.

Specifying your business's capital requirements

Whether your project is a business expansion or a new venture, the readers of your business plan will want to know what capital investment is required.

How much money do you need to raise, how much do you expect from them, and how do you intend to use the money?

Tip: Don't plan on overburdening the business with too much debt. Debt can seem attractive—ready cash!—but too much debt can weigh down a company's ability to grow.

For Private Communications Corporation's financial plan, Laszlo opens by stating the capital requirements—how much money they are seeking—and how the money will be used (for system development, marketing expenses, partner acquisition programs, etc.).

Financial Plan

Capital requirements

The Company is presently seeking to raise the sum of Two Hundred and Fifty Thousand Dollars ($250,000). According to current projections, the Company believes that these proceeds, together with Eighty-Four Thousand Dollars ($84,000) the Company has already raised in its initial round of financing, will be sufficient to achieve its business plan. After the first six months of operation, the Company will be able to fund all operation, marketing, and product development costs internally.

The Company intends to use the $334,000 during the first six months of operation, as shown below:

- $45,000 for system development and programming
- $200,000 for marketing expenses
- $89,000 for working capital to fund future product development, promotion, and partner acquisition programs

Summary financial projections

The financial plan portrays a projection of first-year sales of $11.74 million, gross margins over 60 percent, and net margins of approximately 42 percent before tax. The Company expects to be profitable after the first six months of operation and remain profitable from that point on. Other expenses are budgeted as a percentage of revenues according to similar industry ratios. Given these projected numbers, the Company anticipates being profitable and cash flow positive within six months of Product launch. The important results of the financial forecast are summarized below:

	2010	2011	2012	2013	2014
Revenue ($)	11,744,628	33,826,076	39,624,551	43,587,006	47,945,706
Operating profit ($)	4,923,821	14,549,719	16,963,578	18,723,261	20,660,335
Operating margin	42%	43%	43%	43%	43%
Net income ($)	4,922,779	14,547,754	16,963,451	18,723,180	20,660,302
Net margin	42%	43%	43%	43%	43%

Providing financial projections

In this section, you should highlight and explain the importance of the significant figures from the pro forma income statements—revenue, operating profit, operating margin, net income, net margin—over a period of three to five years. State when you expect the company or project to become profitable.

Tip: Do the number crunching yourself. Even if you are not a numbers person and have expert advice, get in there and do the gritty work of building an income statement and balance sheet.

The pro forma financial statements are projected statements—what you believe will be the future income. They represent your most honest analysis of the financial progress of the business. The income statement, also know as the profit and loss statement, shows the profit margins. The balance sheet provides a picture of the business's assets, equities, and liabilities at a specific point in time.

In addition to the income statement summary, most of your readers will be concerned with the cash flow statement. Including a summary of the flow of cash, showing the times of peak need and peak availability, will demonstrate that your plan has accounted for the variability of cash flows.

Tip: If your new business is a start-up venture, pay especially close attention to cash flow in your financial plan. Although most people think of profits first, cash flow can be more important for a start-up.

Cash flow is often presented on a quarterly or monthly basis.

Articulating your assumptions

State your assumptions about the estimated industry and market growth rates. Then give your assumptions about the internal variables of the business, such as the variable and fixed costs, growth rate of sales, cost of capital, and seasonal cash flow fluctuations.

Your assumptions are the underpinnings of your financial plan. They should be realistic, within the bounds of industry experience. Include a more detailed set of assumptions as an attachment. Be sure to document your assumptions. Give your sources, evidence, expert opinions, and your own logic for choosing a certain growth rate or cost for distribution. PCC's assumptions are show below.

Assumptions

The financial projections are based on current industry estimates of Internet and proprietary OSP subscribers, primary and secondary market research data, and estimates of the Product's market penetration and sales growth. More detailed information on the assumptions can be found in the statements prepared for years 2010 through 2014. These statements include projected income statements, balance sheets, and cash flows, as well as a detailed breakdown of assumptions.

Revenues include those resulting from registration of new accounts and sales of additional calling minutes. Cost of goods sold, while calculated on a per-minute rate, includes all services associated with buying, selling, and billing the customer for long-distance time, as well as all fees and chargebacks associated with credit card billing. Marketing and sales expenses include costs associated with advertising, PR, and promotions, as well as those from revenue sharing with strategic partners. The company will not carry any inventory and will operate with minimal overhead, due to the nature of the business.

Conducting breakeven analysis for sales

As you saw earlier, the breakeven point is the time when the business or project is neither losing nor gaining money. This is the pivotal moment when the business begins to be profitable. Will it take six months or two years for the business venture to reach its breakeven? The reader of your business plan will want to know when and at what level of sales the breakeven point will occur.

The breakeven point for sales is calculated as follows:

where fixed costs are those costs that don't change as sales go up or down (for

$$\text{Breakeven} = \frac{\text{Fixed Cost}}{(\text{Sales} - \text{Variable Costs})/\text{Sales}}$$

example, rental of

facilities), and variable costs vary in proportion to sales (for example, raw materials). This calculation could be included in the attachments to your business plan.

Assessing risk and reward

Risk is the uncertainty of the future. Even with the most careful planning and judicious assumptions, you cannot predict what will happen tomorrow or next month or next year. Planning at all levels—understanding the business environment, developing the operations plan and the marketing plan—is the best way to reduce a venture's exposure to risk, but you can never completely eliminate risk.

FIGURE 1

Risk/return graph

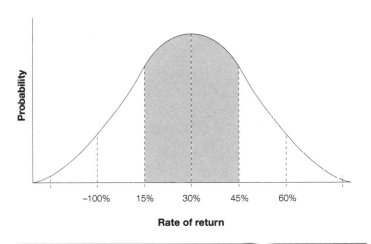

There is real risk in any venture—the risk of failure and the possibility of reward. Your readers will want to know your assessment of the level of risk. They want to know how you plan to avoid the risk of failure and how you plan to increase the chances for success. A risk/return graph can quickly show your readers the likelihood of failure, of achieving the predicted levels of return, and the chance of phenomenal success.

The risk/return graph shows investors the probability of possible outcomes. The risk of losing everything is very low, as is the chance of a very high return. The most likely outcome is indicated by the area under the bell curve, ranging from an acceptable (perhaps) return of 15 percent to the most likely return of 30 percent and a possible 45 percent rate of return. Depending on the fundamental riskiness of the venture (drilling for oil is riskier than opening a retail clothes store), the investor will require different rates of return to balance the possibility of loss (an investor investing in oil drilling would expect a high return to compensate for the risk of loss).

Anticipating financial returns

Investors also want to know the expected financial returns—typically either the return on investment (ROI) or the internal rate of return (IRR). For an internal project, the financial return should exceed the company's hurdle rate—the minimum rate of return expected of all projects. For a risky start-up business, investors generally require a higher return to compensate for the higher level of risk of loss.

To calculate the ROI, divide net operating income by total investments. For example:

$$\$45,000 / \$300,000 = 0.15 \text{ or } 15\% \text{ ROI}$$

The higher the ROI, the more efficient the company is in using its capital to produce a profit.

To calculate an IRR of 50 percent—the return an investor might expect for a risky investment—use the following formula:

$$FV = \text{investment} \times (1 + 0.5)^n$$

where FV is future value, *investment* is the dollar amount of the investment, and n is the number of years to receive the return.

The complete set of financial information—assumptions, income statements, cash flow statements, balance sheets, statement of sources and uses—should be included in the attachments to your business plan.

Preparing a Budget

An Overview of Budgeting

A S A MANAGER, you may be asked to prepare a budget for your department or business unit. But what is a budget, exactly? How does budgeting work, and why is preparing a well-thought-out budget important? Let's take a closer look at these questions below.

What is a budget?

A *budget* is the financial blueprint or action plan for a department or organization. It translates strategic plans into measurable expenditures and anticipated returns over a certain period of time.

Budgeting activities include:

- Forecasting future business results, such as sales volume, revenues, capital investments, and expenses

- Reconciling those forecasts to organizational goals and financial constraints

- Obtaining organizational support for your proposed budget

- Managing subsequent business activities to achieve budgeted results

If you have profit and loss responsibility, the difference between the financial results of your division or business unit and the budget may be a key factor in evaluating your job performance. This difference may also be tied to your compensation.

An understanding of the basics of budgeting and the budget process is, therefore, essential to creating realistic budgets that will later serve as performance benchmarks. Moreover, if you are skilled at "selling the budget" within your organization and negotiating compromises during the budgeting process, you will be more likely to see your budget requests met.

How does the budgeting process work?

The process of preparing a budget involves establishing goals, evaluating different strategies for achieving these goals, and assessing the financial impacts of these strategies. There are typically four components in the budget-preparation process.

1. **Setting goals.** Some organizations mandate companywide goals, such as "Increase net profits by 10 percent during the next year." Individual departments then translate these directives into financial goals that are relevant for their particular activities. For example, the sales department might set a goal of increasing revenues, while the purchasing department will look for ways to reduce costs.

2. **Evaluating and choosing options.** Several tactics—such as launching a new marketing campaign to drive sales, finding a lower-cost supplier to reduce expenses, and hiring more employees to improve customer service—may be used to meet a specific goal. You will need to consider which tactics are likely

to be most effective in your particular situation and which will also be supported across the organization. After all, a great idea is just that—an idea—if you don't get approval to implement it.

3. **Identifying budget impacts.** Decisions about strategic goals and tactics are used to develop assumptions about future costs and revenues. For example, upgrading your advertising to reach more markets might mean that you need to hire professional marketing consultants.

4. **Coordinating departmental budgets.** Individual unit and division budgets are combined into a single master budget that expresses the organization's overall financial objectives and strategic goals.

Typically, preparing budgets is an iterative process in which different groups create preliminary budgets and then come together to identify and resolve differences.

Why is a budget valuable?

Budgets can serve as essential tools for measuring managers' performance. By comparing actual business results to the budget over a period of time, an evaluator can determine a manager's overall success in achieving his or her department's strategic goals.

Of course, actual results may differ from budgeted results due to reasons beyond an individual manager's control—such as an overall downturn in the economic cycle or an unexpected spike in prices of raw materials. Thus anyone using a budget to evaluate a manager's performance should be sure that the performance evaluations are matched to appropriate measures of results.

Many different financial measures of managerial performance can be drawn from comparing budgeted to actual business results. Here are a few examples:

- *Gross margin* measures profitability after direct production costs but before other costs that are not specifically tied to production, such as marketing, administrative, and interest expenses. For example:

  Gross margin = $40,000/$120,000 = 33%

- *SG&A* (selling, general, and administrative costs) as a percentage of sales is a measure of a department's or organization's effectiveness in controlling costs. For instance:

  SG&A as a percentage of sales = $20,000/$120,000 = 16.7%

- *Revenue per employee* is a measure of the operational efficiency of a department or organization, relative to other units or companies in the same industry. To illustrate:

  Revenue per employee = $120,000,000/225 = $533,333

These and other measures can help an organization evaluate the effectiveness of its managers.

Types of budgets

There are different types of budgets for different purposes. Some of the main types of budgets include the following:

- *Operating budgets* reflect day-to-day expenses and depreciation (the current portion of capitalized expenses). They typically cover a one-year period. Department, division, and unit managers are usually asked to come up with operating budgets for their part of the business.

- *Capital budgets* show planned outlays for investments in plant, equipment, and product development. Capital budgets may cover periods of three, five, or ten years. Again, managers throughout an organization may be expected to prepare this type of budget.

- *Cash budgets* plot the expected cash balances the organization will experience during the forecast period, based on information provided in operating and capital budgets. Cash budgets are prepared by an organization's finance department and are critical to ensuring that the company has sufficient liquidity (cash and credit) available to meet expected cash disbursements.

- *Master budgets* reflect the aggregation of department, division, and business unit budgets. As we've seen, department or unit managers are most frequently asked to develop operating budgets and capital budgets for their departments. You can also create subsets of the operating and capital budgets for individual projects, geographic locations, or large, line item expenses such as advertising. These detailed schedules allow you to keep a closer eye on revenues and expenses within your department. Departmental operating and capital budgets are coordinated to create *financial budgets* including the cash budget, the budgeted balance sheet, and the budgeted statement of cash flows. All of these budgets together are then "rolled up into" the master budget, summarizing the financial projections within an organization for a given period of time. See the illustration "Coordinating departmental budgets into the master budget" for an example of how this works.

Steps for Preparing a Cash Budget

A cash budget helps ensure that your organization, division, or department will have the cash necessary to function throughout the budget period. The cash budget can be broken down into smaller units—months or quarters, for example—within the entire budget period to reflect changing cash flows.

1. **Determine the beginning cash balance.** Determine how much cash will be available at the beginning of the period (fiscal year or quarter or month).

2. **Add receipts.** Determine the expected receipts—collections from customers—that will flow into the cash account each period. Cash collections may vary during the budget period. For example, many retail stores expect to receive most of their receipts during holiday seasons.

3. **Deduct disbursements.** According to expected activity, calculate how much cash will be required to cover disbursements—cash payouts—during the period. Disbursements could include payment for materials, payroll, taxes due, and so on. Some of these expenditures may be evenly distributed throughout the budget period, but some, such as payroll or material costs, may fluctuate as part of the production process.

4. **Calculate the cash excess or deficiency.** To calculate the cash excess or deficiency for a period, subtract the disbursement from the sum of the beginning cash balance and the receipts expected during that period.

5. **Determine financing needed.** To calculate the cash excess or deficiency for a period, subtract the disbursement from total cash available. If, at the end of the period, there is a cash excess, then financing of operations may be covered by the available cash. If, on the other hand, there is a cash deficiency, then you have to plan on financing the period's cash needs from other sources, such as a bank loan. Note: remember to include a stable cash balance beyond the immediate cash needs. For example, a manufacturing division may want to maintain a $30,000 cash balance at all times to cover unexpected cash demands. When you borrow money for operating expenses, you need to establish a payback schedule. For each period, include the repayment of loan principal and interest in the cash budget.

6. **Establish the ending cash balance.** The ending cash balance for each period will include the receipts and loans less the disbursements and financing costs. The ending cash balance becomes the beginning cash balance for the next period.

Coordinating departmental budgets into the master budget

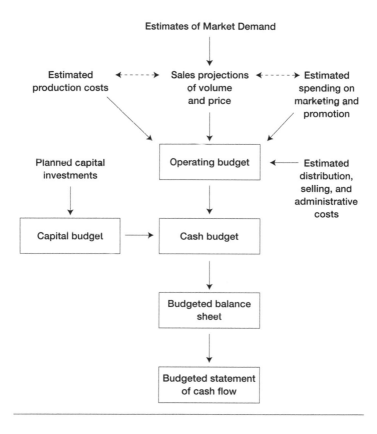

Approaches to Preparing a Budget

HOW DO YOU APPROACH preparing budgets needed for your part of the organization? You have several options at your disposal. Below, we examine a few different approaches.

Traditional budgeting

Many organizations use a "traditional" budget—a budget that covers a one-year period and that presents forecasts that do not change during the life of the budget cycle. Companies use traditional budgets because they are easy to put together and they simplify coordination of budget assumptions across different departments.

Traditional budgets, however, have been under growing attack from those who feel that they no longer serve a modern organization's needs. Critics complain that such budgets are timed incorrectly (too long or too short); rely on inappropriate measures; and are too simplistic (or too complex), too rigid (inflexible in a changing business environment), or too political (the incentives for managers send the wrong messages).

As a result, some organizations blend alternative approaches to budgeting to meet their individual needs. Below, the traditional approach is contrasted with alternative approaches.

Alternative approaches

The table "Traditional budgets and alternative approaches" shows the elements of a traditional budget and some alternative approaches to budgeting that your company may use.

While the alternative approaches may result in greater accuracy and functionality, they also have their disadvantages. For example, some (such as zero-based budgeting) can consume so much time that they distract managers from other critical activities.

Kaizen budgeting

If your company uses *Kaizen budgeting*, cost reductions are built into the budget on an incremental basis so that continual efforts are made to reduce costs over a given time period. The advantage of Kaizen budgeting is that the budget process puts continuous pressure on managers to achieve cost efficiencies. A disadvantage is that Kaizen budgeting is difficult to maintain because the rate of budgeted cost reduction declines over time, making it more difficult to achieve improvements after the "easy" changes have been achieved.

Budgeting and the balanced scorecard

For the most part, traditional budgeting has focused on the financial performance of an organization. However, many of these financial performance measures, designed to indicate the success of budget plans in contributing to increasing profits, were developed for an industrial world.

What Would YOU Do?

Feeding the Dragon

MEI PO RUNS Gift of the Dragon, a small artisan shop that makes decorations and gifts for the Chinese New Year. Unique handcrafted touches and a great word-of-mouth reputation keep her products in high demand.

Recently, Mei Po learned that the space next door was available to lease. The timing was right as she was looking to expand her business. But as she reviewed the loan application, she noticed that in addition to a business plan, she needed to prepare a one-year budget. Mei Po was taken aback.

She planned her cash flow month to month. How could she predict what would happen over the period of a year? It seemed impossible. She wondered where to even start.

What would YOU do? See *What You COULD Do.*

Times have changed, and new ways of approaching planning and performance evaluation have changed as well. With information technology and global markets becoming the model for the modern business environment, and as nonprofit organizations grow in size and sophistication, organizations have to recognize

Traditional budgets and alternative approaches

Budget parameter	Approach	Description
Time period of the budget	Fixed budget (traditional)	The budget period is a specific time period, usually coinciding with the company's fiscal year.
	Rolling budget	The budget is continuously updated so that the time frame remains stable while the actual period covered by the budget changes. For example, as each month passes, a one-year rolling budget would be extended by one month so that there would always be a one-year budget in place.
Forecast values	Static budget (traditional)	Presents one forecast for a given time period and is not changed during the life of the budget.
	Flexible budget	Budgeted revenues and costs are adjusted during the budget period according to pre-determined variances between the budgeted and actual output and revenue.
Forecasting process	Incremental budgeting (traditional)	The previous period's budget and actual results, as well as expectations for the future, are used in determining the budget for the next period.
	Zero-based budgeting	The budgeting process begins from the ground up, as though the budget were being prepared for the first time.
Setting goals	Top-down budgeting (traditional)	Senior management sets budget goals—such as revenue and profit—and imposes these goals on the rest of the organization.
	Participatory budgeting	Those responsible for achieving the budget goals are included in setting those goals.

and value their intangible and intellectual assets as well as the tangible assets represented in numbers on the balance sheet.

The *balanced scorecard* is a way for managers to view their organization from four interrelated perspectives of operational drivers for future performance:

1. **Financial perspective.** How are we doing using traditional financial performance measures? How do shareholders view us?

2. **Customer perspective.** How satisfied, loyal, and profitable are our customers?

3. **Internal process perspective.** What internal business processes do we excel at, and which processes do we need to improve?

4. **Learning and growth perspective.** How can we build a workforce that is constantly learning and improving, so that employees excel at their jobs in ways that delight customers and generate the financial results our company needs?

The balanced scorecard gives upper management a quick and effective view of the critical factors affecting the organization's performance now and in the future. The methodology also puts the strategic mission, rather than financial controls, at the center of the budget-preparation process.

The balanced scorecard is linked to the budget process in the following ways:

- It highlights leading indicators, such as new product development, customer complaints, or direct mail response rates, instead of only sales or cost figures.

- It balances the four perspectives. Thus, for example, pressure to develop new products doesn't overshadow the need for quality products and customer satisfaction.

- It helps management to communicate strategic goals and the organization's mission to all the stakeholders in the enterprise.

To build a balanced scorecard, managers follow these steps:

- **Develop goals and measures for critical financial performance measures.** In other words, prepare a budget as a financial action plan.

- **Develop goals and measures for critical customer performance variables.** Managers first identify the target market, and then they develop ways to measure variables such as customer loyalty through repeat buying, response rates, new customer referrals, customer complaints, and price sensitivity. The focus is on identifying ways to retain current customers, increase levels of customer purchases, increase levels of profitability per customer, and acquire new customers.

- **Develop goals and measures for critical internal process performance variables.** Managers look at the three areas of internal process:

  1. The innovation cycle or research, development, and design of products and service

  2. The operations cycle in which the products are manufactured and delivered or services are rendered

3. The postsale service cycle in which customer service is the primary activity

   Each of these internal process areas relates directly to both financial performance and customer satisfaction.

- **Develop goals and measures for critical learning, and growth performance measures.** Here managers step back to consider the infrastructure and capabilities needed for the organization to create the long-term growth the strategic mission envisions. Growth will occur through human resources, systems, and organizational procedures. This perspective clarifies the investment decisions management has to make to achieve its goals. Will the organization have to invest in training people? In hiring more people for specific roles? In improving its technology systems? Empowering employees—encouraging employee loyalty—and aligning organizational structures to meet the company's changing needs simultaneously enhance the ability of the organization in the other three critical areas.

The key to linking the balanced scorecard is to develop the performance measures or drivers that can help predict future outcomes. The balanced scorecard provides the guidance for planning—the budget—which, in turn, provides feedback and allows for course correction as the time period stipulated in the budget advances. This provides information managers can use to translate the strategic vision into reality and to constanty improve the budget-preparation process.

What You COULD Do.

Remember Mei Po's concern about how to begin preparing her one-year budget?

The first step in developing a budget is to establish a set of assumptions about the future. Questions Mei Po might ask include, Will the demand for her gifts grow over the next year? If yes, by how much? The next step is for Mei Po to calculate expected revenues and expenses based on past performance and future expectations. The difference between revenues and expenses is net income. If Mei Po is satisfied with the numbers, she can finalize her budget. If she wants higher net income, she needs to identify new strategies that will support different assumptions.

Categorizing Expenses

A BIG PART OF preparing any budget is anticipating and categorizing various types of expenses. Below are some suggestions for making sure you've covered all the bases when it comes to expenses for your department or unit.

Fixed and variable costs

In preparing budgets, you need to differentiate between fixed costs and variable costs. *Fixed costs* are those that remain fairly constant within a wide range of production or sales volumes. Examples of fixed costs include:

- Rent
- Basic utilities, including electric and telephone service
- Equipment leases
- Depreciation
- Interest payments
- Administrative costs
- Marketing and advertising
- Indirect labor, such as salaried supervisory employees

Variable costs are those that change in direct proportion to changes in activity. Examples of variable costs include:

- Raw materials

- Direct labor

- Packaging

- Depreciation due to usage

- Power and gas used in manufacturing

- Shipping

- Sales commissions

- Income taxes

Estimates of variable costs that will be incurred during the budget period will depend on the production forecast you come up with for your unit or department. On the surface some costs may appear fixed. In reality, however, they represent long-term variable costs. For example, if production or sales volumes increase by a sufficiently large amount, a company may need to lease additional equipment, rent more warehouse space, or hire additional administrative help. Being aware of such requirements will enable you to anticipate the need for expanded capacity and to include these expenditures in your budget requests.

Allocated costs

Operating budgets may include *allocated costs*—costs associated with operating the overall company that are not tied to individual products or departments. The most significant allocation is usually overhead. This figure typically includes the office rent for the

What Would YOU Do?

Smooth Operator?

ELKE HAS RECENTLY become manager of the shoe division of LifeSport, a sportswear manufacturing company. Today, she and LifeSport's other division managers are meeting with their boss, Ahmed, to begin planning next year's division budgets.

During the meeting, Ahmed states LifeSport's strategic goals for next year. "Our industry has been quite stable," he says. "For this year, I'd like to see if all our divisions can boost their operating income by 10 percent, without increasing costs any more than they have to." Ahmed then encourages the managers to use the budget-preparation experience to deepen their understanding of marketplace realities.

Elke returns to her office, thinking about what approach she should take to creating a budget that achieves Ahmed's strategic goals. Should she take last year's operating income for her division and project the desired 10 percent increase for the upcoming year? What about creating a plan that calls for monthly (rather than quarterly) reviews and updates to the budget, so she can react to marketplace realities? Should she instead ask various managers throughout LifeSport what market trends they expect to see next year? It all seems so complicated.

What would YOU do? See *What You COULD Do*.

building occupied by corporate headquarters, and salaries and expenses associated with corporate management.

How these costs are attributed to individual departments varies from one company to another. Some organizations may allocate overhead to certain department budgets—those that produce revenue, for example—and not others.

Activity-based costing

Your company may use *activity-based costing (ABC)* to allocate costs. Activity-based costing allows companies to more precisely identify overhead costs associated with producing revenue. Instead of allocating overhead costs to products based on broad measures such as revenue or production volume, ABC starts with the cost of resources, allocates these costs to activities, and then allocates the cost of activities to products. Activities may be broadly defined (such as managing purchasing) or narrowly defined (such as managing purchasing for research and development). Maintaining an ABC system requires managers and employees to gather detailed information about how much of their time is devoted to particular activities.

Activity-based budgeting

Organizations that use ABC to allocate overhead and other costs to individual departments may also adopt *activity-based budgeting (ABB)*. Activity-based budgeting starts with forecasting the planned sales volume for each product. Historical data from the activity-based costing system is then used to estimate the required activities to produce that volume, the resources required to support those activities, and the cost of those resources. The illustration "Inverse relationship between ABC and ABB" shows an example.

Inverse relationship between ABC and ABB

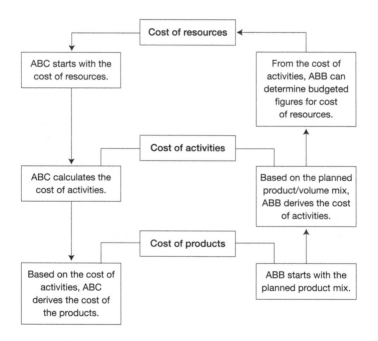

Source: Adapted from Robert S. Kaplan and Robin Cooper, *Cost and Effect: Using Integrated Cost Systems to Drive Profitability and Performance* (Boston: Harvard Business School Press, 1998).

The primary advantage of activity-based budgets is that costs can be more accurately associated with activities, making the planning process more precise and corrections more effective. Companies using this approach report benefits including:

- Establishing more realistic budgets
- Improved accuracy in identifying resource needs
- Better linking of costs to outputs
- More precise allocation of costs to staff responsibilities

The disadvantage of this approach is that it can be costly and complex to establish. Thus it may not be worth the trouble for a small company with few products or services. It also has to be adopted by and embedded into the whole organization; one division alone can't decide to develop its own ABC or ABB system. But when the circumstances are right, activity-based approaches to understanding the economic dynamics of an organization provide long-term planning benefits.

?What You COULD Do.

Remember Elke's uncertainty about how to prepare an operating budget for her division that supports the company's new strategic goal?

Elke should start by asking the finance manager, purchasing group, and other managers throughout LifeSport what market trends they expect to see next year. It's valuable to begin the process of preparing any budget by making *assumptions* about the future. For example, Elke will need to estimate whether the market will grow next year, how customers will respond to new products or features, and what competitors will be doing. Then she'll have to make projections about revenues and other budget figures for her division based on that data.

To establish these assumptions, she should gather information from the financial group (they have estimates of future economic trends), human resources (they understand labor market shifts), sales reps (they know consumer trends), and purchasing (they have news about suppliers).

This is a far better step than taking last year's operating income for her division and merely projecting the desired 10 percent increase for the coming year. Though many companies use historical figures to extrapolate subsequent budgets, this approach doesn't encourage managers to evaluate the realities of the current and future marketplace—something Ahmed stressed during the meeting. Also, it encourages some managers to develop a "use it or lose it" point of view. They feel they must use all of their budgeted expenditures by the end of the period so the next period's budget won't be reduced by the amount that would have been saved.

Preparing an Operating Budget

Now let's turn to how you might prepare an operating budget for your department or unit. To prepare such a budget, you need to take eight steps:

- Defining your goals
- Articulating your assumptions
- Forecasting sales
- Forecasting revenues
- Forecasting cost of goods sold
- Estimating SG&A costs
- Calculating operating income
- Exploring "what-if" scenarios

Below, we look at each of these steps more closely.

Defining your goals

Some goals may be set by senior management, while others are determined by the managers of individual departments or units. These goals will reflect both the organization's larger strategic priorities and the department's or business unit's tactical goals. Examples of questions you might ask to help define your department's tactical goals include:

- What technological changes are affecting our industry?

- How can our current business processes be improved?

- What longer-term initiatives should we consider in order to position our company to compete successfully in the future?

Achieving these goals requires choosing tactics that may in turn affect the budget. The table "Examples of goals, options, and budget impacts" provides an illustration.

Examples of goals, options, and budget impacts

Goal	Options	Budget impacts
Become the most reliable provider of Internet services	Maintain state-of-the-art equipment	Capital investment
	Train the most skilled repair teams in the field	Higher labor and training costs
	Provide the most timely customer service	Increased spending on customer support
Increase revenues by 10%	Raise prices	Lower sales volume, higher gross margin
	Expand marketing	Increased sales, higher marketing costs, increased production costs
	Enter into partnerships	Increased revenues, higher production costs, higher selling costs

What Would YOU Do?

No Day at the Beach

I<small>T'S</small> N<small>OVEMBER</small>. And Jorge is under pressure. He's trying to forecast next year's sales at his Los Angeles–based beach ball company, Beachy Keen. This past year was rough. El Nino (the seasonal warming of the tide) caused larger-than-usual waves in southern California. People filled amusement parks instead of beaches. Luckily, next year's weather is predicted to be back to normal—and Jorge plans to seize the opportunity to launch a new marketing campaign.

He mulls over what data he should use to forecast next year's sales. First, he considers using the run rate. He also evaluates the potential of using the past year's projected annual sales. And he weights the possibility of using the past year's projected annual sales plus 25 percent. Each option seems to offer valuable information, so he's not sure what to do.

What would YOU do? See *What You COULD Do*.

Articulating your assumptions

Whenever you prepare a budget, you have to make some assumptions about the future. In many companies, senior management will communicate key assumptions that are to be used throughout the organization—such as a 5 percent increase in salaries or a 10 percent increase in sales volumes. In other cases, the assumptions are specific to each department's activities.

Managers use a wide variety of data and approaches to articulate their assumptions, including historical trends, purchasing surveys, and industry projections. They also communicate with each other about their expectations for customer response, supplier performance, financial market fluctuation, and so on. Be sure to document all of your assumptions, and keep notes of sources of information you use.

"Unless we find some way to keep our sights on tomorrow, we cannot expect to be in touch with today."
—Dean Rusk

Tips for Setting Assumptions

- Use historical data as a starting point. Even when times are changing quickly, information about past performance can establish a base from which to begin.
- Trust your own experience. Make educated guesses about what is likely to happen in the future.
- Listen to your intuition. Even though you can't verify those gut feelings, you can take them into account.
- Do due diligence. Go out and get the information you need. This may involve doing research, reading trade journals, collecting industry statistics, and so on. And don't forget that the Internet is a growing information resource.

- Talk with and listen to knowledgeable people. Discuss your ideas with team members, colleagues, mentors. Seek out industry participants, suppliers, concerned community leaders, and experts in the field. Engage in discussions with competitors.
- Learn when to be a risk taker and when to be conservative. In a volatile market, conservative assumptions may be the safest.
- Test your assumptions. If possible, try out your assumptions in small experiments before you accept them.

Forecasting sales

Sales projections for a given period are developed by product or product group. If you are forecasting product sales, consider whether it is appropriate to base your forecasts on current sales trends. Some factors to consider, in addition to overall demand trends for these types of products, are:

- The history of sales growth for your company's products

- Competitive products that have been or may be introduced in the market

- Availability of substitute products (for example, if your company sells carbonated beverages, tea and coffee may be substitute products)

- Price sensitivity of purchasers (that is, will a slight increase in price drive customers away?)

- Percentage of customers who make repeat purchases
- Planned changes in sales and promotion activities

If you use historical sales data as a base for your sales forecasts, determine whether it is appropriate to use annual data or the run rate.

The *run rate* is the extrapolation of current financial results out over a future period of time. For example, if December's sales are $75,000, the annual run rate ($75,000 multiplied by twelve months) is $900,000.

Annual data may be most appropriate for forecasting one-off product sales, while the run rate may be better if you are forecasting revenues for services sold under long-term contracts or for recently launched products.

In the examples on the two next pages, the company sells products and also sells monthly services under long-term contracts. The table "Forecasting revenues using the run rate for product and contract sales" shows projected sales for year 2 using the run rate from year 1. The table "Forecasting revenues at 110 percent of total year 1 product and contract sales" shows projected sales for year 2 assuming a 10 percent increase over total sales from year 1.

For products, the examples assume that sales are fairly evenly distributed over the course of year 1, so there is little difference between the two approaches ($900,000 versus $965,800). However, if product sales were concentrated in only a few months of the year, using the run rate would grossly over- or underestimate product revenues for year 2.

Forecasting revenues using the run rate for product and contract sales

	Dec. year 1 sales	Year 2 total projected sales @ Dec. year 1 run rate
Product sales	$75,000	$900,000
Contract monthly services sales:		
Client A (added Jan. year 1)	$4,000	$48,000
Client B (added Apr. year 1)	$4,000	$48,000
Client C (added Oct. year 1)	$6,000	$72,000
Client D (added Dec. year 1)	$9,000	$108,000
Subtotal contract services sales:	**$23,000**	**$276,000**
Total revenue:	$98,000	$1,176,000

Projections for contract services in the example are more realistic when the run rate is used ($276,000) because many new contracts signed in year 1 were signed late in the year. Using annual data for contract services results in a very conservative estimate ($122,100) for year 2.

The most realistic revenue forecast for this company, and the revenue figure that will be used in subsequent examples, is $1,241,800. This amount is based on 110 percent of year 1 product sales, plus the December run rate for contract services.

Forecasting revenues at 110 percent of total year 1 product and contract sales

	Year 1 total sales	Year 2 total projected sales @ 110% of year 1 total sales
Product sales	$878,000	$965,800
Contract monthly services sales:		
Client A (added Jan. year 1)	$48,000	$52,800
Client B (added Apr. year 1)	$36,000	$39,600
Client C (added Oct. year 1)	$18,000	$19,800
Client D (added Dec. year 1)	$9,000	$9,900
Subtotal contract services sales:	**$111,000**	**$122,100**
Total revenue:	$939,000	$1,087,900

Forecasting revenues

Historical data, existing order backlogs, and information about the sales pipeline can help you estimate how new sales volume might be distributed during the budget period. If necessary, create a monthly schedule to clarify how sales volumes and revenues are expected to fluctuate during the year. Doing so will help prevent overly optimistic forecasts. This is important, because it's all too easy to let overoptimism distort your forecasts. David Michels, former group chief executive of the Hilton Group, offered some valuable insights into this issue:

> *One of the strangest things that I've encountered in all the businesses I've been in, and ever since I've been in business, is that I can rarely remember anyone—whether it's in betting hotels, holiday camps, bingo or machine sales—ever bringing me a five-year forecast (which is what most people ask for) where business wasn't always better in the fifth year.*
>
> *What you normally get, which is quite infamous, is the wonderful "hockey stick" forecast, where perhaps business isn't wonderful now so the graph comes down a bit. Then for the next four years it goes up, and the ending is always Y percentage higher than the beginning. First, one needs to understand why people do that. You're presenting something that might be your own job, your own idea, your own division, your own department or your own business to your boss or a committee of bosses. Very few people want to sit in front of them saying: "OK chaps, I'm going to do much worse in five years than I am now. Can I have a raise?" So, it's very important to remember that.*
>
> *The other thing is that people are natural optimists: really, most of us are. If you ask people "Will the weather be better next month than it is this month?" nine out of ten people will tell you "yes," because they want it to be—not because they necessarily believe it will be.*

And if you ask: "Will business be better next month or in five years' time?" most people will say "Yes"; not because they believe it will be but because they want it to be. It's just natural human emotion.

Since revenues are a function of units sold and price, you will want to document quantity and price assumptions used in developing your revenue forecast. Be aware that production constraints may affect the revenue budget. If, for example, you expect sales demand to exceed capacity, then you'll need to adjust the revenue budget to match the production constraints rather than the actual demands of the market.

Be prepared to defend your assumptions, especially if you are also evaluated based on achieving your budgeted revenue targets.

Forecasting cost of goods sold

After defining your goals, articulating your assumptions, and forecasting sales and revenues, the next step in preparing your operating budget is to estimate costs associated with those revenues. One of those is the cost of goods sold.

These costs include materials, labor, other direct product costs, and manufacturing overhead. You estimate them based on units of product or, for a service company, hours of service. In forecasting cost of goods sold, consider the expected sales volume as well as planned changes in inventory. For example, if inventories are depleted at the beginning of the budget period, additional production will be required to bring inventories up to normal levels,

Cost of goods sold: year 2 budget

	Actual Year 1	Year 2 budget	Rate of change
Cost of goods sold:			
Direct labor	$192,325	$256,500	33.4%
Overhead	$6,755	$7,200	7.0%
Direct materials	$111,000	$119,000	7.2%
Total cost of goods sold	**$310,080**	**$382,700**	**23.4%**

increasing total direct production costs. Conversely, excess inventory will be worked off during the period, reducing forecast production costs.

In estimating line item expenses, be aware of breakpoints in production capacity that signal the need for additional outlays. For example, suppose you currently need three people to produce ten thousand orders a month, and you estimate that during the next year sales will increase by 20 percent to twelve thousand orders. At what point will you need to add additional staff to handle the extra volume? The table "Cost of goods sold: year 2 budget" shows one possible response.

Estimating SG&A costs

Selling, general, and administrative costs are additional costs associated with revenues. They can include costs generated by research and development, product design, marketing, distribution, cus-

SG&A: year 2 budget

	Actual Year 1	Year 2 budget	Rate of change
Sales, general, and administrative costs:			
Sales salaries	$220,000	$291,200	32.4%
Advertising expenses	$45,000	$51,000	13.3%
Miscellaneous selling expenses	$4,200	$3,900	(7.1%)
Office expenses	$92,000	$94,500	2.7%
Total SG&A	**$361,200**	**$440,600**	**22.0%**

tomer service, commissions, administration, and overhead. In the example shown in the table "SG&A: year 2 budget," only marketing and administrative expenses make up the SG&A budget.

Calculating operating income

Now it's time to calculate *operating income*—the difference between expected sales and expected costs—for your budget. The table "Operating income: year 2 budget" shows an example.

In this sample budget, contract service sales resulted in a significant jump in anticipated sales revenues in year 2. However, sales salaries and direct labor costs rose in proportion. The projected growth in operating income is largely due to the assumption that overhead and direct materials costs would not be affected by the increase in contract sales.

Operating income: year 2 budget

	Actual Year 1	Year 2 budget	Rate of change
Operating income:			
Total revenue	**$939,000**	**$1,241,800**	**32.2%**
Cost of goods sold	$310,080	$382,700	23.4%
SG&A	$361,200	$440,600	22.0%
Total costs	**$92,000**	**$94,500**	**22.6%**
Total operating income	**$671,280**	**$823,300**	**56.3%**

Exploring "what-if" scenarios

You'll probably have to rework the first draft of your operating budget in order to bring the budgeted results in line with your company's and department's goals and constraints. Testing different possible scenarios can help you with this part of the process. How will a change in one area affect the expected outcome? What if we increase advertising? How much would that increase sales? What if employees decide to go on strike? How can we incorporate that risk into the budget?

A budget is an action plan based on the best available information and assumptions for the future. Performing a sensitivity analysis to test those assumptions or alternative options can greatly enhance the value of budgets as tools for planning and for feedback and course correction.

A sensitivity analysis applies a "what-if" situation to the budget model to see the effect of a potential change on the original data.

For example, what if the cost of materials rises 5 percent, or what if sales rise 10 percent? Calculations for sensitivity analysis can be complicated when dealing with a master budget that has summarized multiple divisional and/or functional budgets. Software packages for financial planning models are available and commonly used to perform these calculations, giving managers a powerful tool to determine the costs and benefits of various options and possibilities.

Using scenario analysis software, you can quickly see the potential impact of a change in assumptions, without having to generate new forecasts for each budget item, such as raw materials or selling and administrative costs. The table "Example of sensitivity analysis" shows how sensitivity analyses for one company might be reported.

Example of sensitivity analysis

What-if scenario	Units sold	Direct materials cost	Operating income
Budget	21,400	$214,000	$383,950
Scenario 1: increase unit sales 10%:	23,540	$203,300	$360,900
Scenario 2: decrease unit sales 5%:	20,330	$6,000	$6,000
Scenario 3: decrease materials cost 5%:	21,400	$203,300	$398,700

Tips for Negotiating Your Team's Budget

- Make sure you understand your organization's budgeting process. What are the guidelines you need to follow? What is the timing of the budget process? How is the budget used in the organization?

- Communicate often with the controller or finance person in your department. Ask questions about points you don't understand. Get that person's advice about the assumptions your team is making.

- Know what real concerns are driving the people making the decisions about your budget. Then be sure to address those concerns.

- Get buy-in from the decision makers. Spend time educating the finance person or decision maker about your area of the business. That will lay the groundwork for implementing changes later.

- Understand each line item in the budget you're working on. If you don't know what something means or where a number comes from, find out yourself. Walk the floor. Talk to people on the line.

- Have an ongoing discussion with your team throughout the budget period. The more you plan, the more you will be able to respond to unplanned contingencies.

- Avoid unpleasant surprises! As they become available, compare actual figures to the budgeted amounts. If there is a significant or unexpected variance, find out why. And be sure to notify the finance person who needs to know.

What You COULD Do.

Remember Jorge's uncertainty about which data he should use to forecast next year's sales at Beachy Keen?

Jorge should use the past year's projected annual sales plus 25 percent. That's because El Nino caused poor beach conditions and low sales this past year, so higher sales are a reasonable projection for next year. In addition, his new marketing campaign will likely increase revenues.

Using the run rate wouldn't be appropriate in this case. Because beach ball sales are seasonal, using any single month as a base for projections will yield a result that is either too high or too low. Using the past year's projected annual sales would also be an unwise move—again, because El Nino caused poor beach conditions and low sales in the previous year, making higher sales a reasonable projection for next year.

Preparing a Capital Budget

I N ADDITION TO preparing operating budgets for your department or unit, you may need to prepare capital budgets. Let's now examine this type of budget more carefully and consider strategies for preparing one.

What is a capital budget?

A *capital budget* is a schedule that shows planned investments in property, equipment, improvements, and other capital assets over a period of time. These outlays are different from ordinary day-to-day expenses in that they can be capitalized under accepted accounting practices. Instead of having to record the entire expense as a deduction from income in one accounting period, you can spread the capitalized expense out over a period of years. Each year, a portion of the capitalized expense is recorded as depreciation.

If you are asked to submit a capital budget request, you will need to estimate the total expenditure associated with each type of investment. For example, you might have one line item for computers, one for office equipment, and another for furniture. Your budget should also include amounts for related costs such as installation charges, consulting fees, the cost of permits, or service contracts.

A capital budget may show planned investments over several years. The table "Example of a capital budget" illustrates a capital

Example of a capital budget

	Year 1	Year 2	Year 3
IT equipment:			
Computers	$45,000	$15,000	$15,000
Servers	$120,000	$25,000	$25,000
Support service	$26,000	–	$29,000
Furniture and fixtures:			
Office furniture	$28,000	$6,000	$6,000
Renovation costs	$89,000	–	–

budget for a department that is migrating to a new computer system in year 1. The budget shows migration costs expected to be incurred in year 1, and estimated costs in subsequent years based on projected growth.

Capital budgeting techniques

Capital budgeting is slightly different from a capital budget—despite the similarity of the terms! It's the process of identifying the potential return on a given investment to determine whether the investment makes sense and to compare alternative investment options. Capital budgeting thus is a key step in preparing a capital budget.

If many different departments are competing to have projects funded, you may be asked to justify your proposals using capital budgeting techniques. The following steps can help:

1. Prepare a schedule of estimated cash flows that identifies outlays, the timing of those outlays, and the expected cost savings or revenue that will result from the investment. For substantial investments, consider annual cash flows over a period of several years. If an expense will be capitalized, the full outlay is recorded for the year in which it is incurred. Also record the expected tax savings that will result in subsequent years as capitalized items are depreciated.

2. Calculate the *net present value* (NPV) of the cash flows using appropriate interest rates. Net present value is the current value of future cash flows. You calculate it by dividing each future cash flow by the compounded interest rate and then adding up all of the discounted cash flows. You can create a spreadsheet (for situations where cash flows or the interest rates used are different from year to year) or use a financial calculator (if the cash flow and interest rate are constant throughout the period).

   The NPV formula is:

$$\text{Net present value} = \text{Cash flow } (CF) + \frac{CF_1}{(1+i)^1} + \frac{CF_2}{(1+i)^2} + \frac{CF_n}{(1+i)^2}$$

where each CF is a future cash flow, n is the number of years over which the cash flow is expected to occur, and i is the interest rate.

Some experts suggest that the interest rate should be based on the company's cost of capital, while others recommend using a risk-adjusted rate that reflects the uncertainty of the future cash flows. Check with your manager to find out how your company handles this.

3. A positive net present value indicates that the investment will potentially benefit the company, while a negative net present value indicates a losing proposition.

When Your Budget and Reality Differ

BECAUSE ALL BUDGETS are based on assumptions about what might happen in the future, actual business results for the future time period stipulated in a particular budget may not reflect what was in the budget. Below are some insights into how you might respond to this situation.

What is variance?

The difference between the actual results produced by your department or unit and the budgeted results you've planned for is called the *variance*. Comparison of actual to budgeted results allows you to consider whether corrective action is needed. The variance can be favorable, when the actual results are better than expected. For example, sales increase more than you anticipated. Or it can be unfavorable, when the actual results are worse than expected. For instance, sales increase less than you anticipated.

Unfavorable variances require corrective action so that future results will be closer to budget. To illustrate, if the increase in sales was less than you had budgeted, you would want to find out why and then address the problem. Was it that salespeople lacked sufficient training in the new products your company was trying to sell? If so, perhaps your department could provide the needed training.

If you cannot affect a particular expense or revenue item, you may be able to compensate by taking action that will cause an offsetting variance in other budget line items. That is, if you have to live with a less-than-ideal increase in sales, perhaps you could cut costs in another area, so that your department's *overall* performance is still good in financial terms.

What causes it?

Sometimes variances are artificially created. For example, if the company's accounting software automatically spreads line item expenses over a twelve-month period and the actual expenditure only occurs once a year, you will have a favorable variance in some months and an unfavorable variance in others.

The table "Possible causes of variance and possible responses" shows examples.

Possible causes of variance and possible responses

Variance	Possible causes	Compensating action
Higher production costs	Increased production volume	None required if increase in production is due to increased sales
	Increase in price of raw materials or labor	Increase selling prices, reduce other expenses
	Timing differences create artificial variance	None required
Lower revenues	Fewer units sold	Reduce fixed expenses and/or increase promotion activities
	Lower selling prices	Reduce expenses or increase selling prices

Tools
and
Resources

Tools and Resources for Understanding Finance

UNDERSTANDING FINANCE

Annual Budgeting and Tracking Worksheet

Use this tool to prepare and track an annual budget with monthly or quarterly revenues and expenses. Enter your annual budget numbers on this sheet in the white cells. Use whole dollars for all entries. Monthly numbers will automatically be calculated on the "Enter Q1, Q2" and "Enter Q3, Q4" sheets that follow. If you would like to alter the monthly numbers in order to show timing of revenues or expenses, do so by simply overwriting the formulas in the monthly budget columns. Use the "Annual Budget Check" columns to make sure that you have not changed the annual totals by reallocating the monthly numbers.

Unit Name _____
Fiscal Year _____
Start Date of Year _January 1, 2005_

	Enter Annual Budget Here	Q1 Budget	Q1 Actual	Q2 Budget	Q2 Actual	Q3 Budget	Q3 Actual	Q4 Budget	Q4 Actual	YTD through Jun-07 Budget	YTD through Jun-07 Actual	YTD Difference	YTD Percent Difference
Revenues													
Source 1		0	0	0	0	0	0	0	0	0	0	0	0%
Source 2		0	0	0	0	0	0	0	0	0	0	0	0%
Source 3		0	0	0	0	0	0	0	0	0	0	0	0%
Source 4		0	0	0	0	0	0	0	0	0	0	0	0%
Source 5		0	0	0	0	0	0	0	0	0	0	0	0%
Source 6		0	0	0	0	0	0	0	0	0	0	0	0%
Total Revenues	0	0	0	0	0	0	0	0	0	0	0	0	0%
Expenses													
Item 1		0	0	0	0	0	0	0	0	0	0	0	0%
Item 2		0	0	0	0	0	0	0	0	0	0	0	0%
Item 3		0	0	0	0	0	0	0	0	0	0	0	0%
Total Category 1	0	0	0	0	0	0	0	0	0	0	0	0	0%
Item 4		0	0	0	0	0	0	0	0	0	0	0	0%
Item 5		0	0	0	0	0	0	0	0	0	0	0	0%
Item 6		0	0	0	0	0	0	0	0	0	0	0	0%
Item 7		0	0	0	0	0	0	0	0	0	0	0	0%
Total Category 2	0	0	0	0	0	0	0	0	0	0	0	0	0%
Item 8		0	0	0	0	0	0	0	0	0	0	0	0%
Item 9		0	0	0	0	0	0	0	0	0	0	0	0%
Item 10		0	0	0	0	0	0	0	0	0	0	0	0%
Total Category 3	0	0	0	0	0	0	0	0	0	0	0	0	0%
Item 11		0	0	0	0	0	0	0	0	0	0	0	0%
Item 12		0	0	0	0	0	0	0	0	0	0	0	0%
Item 13		0	0	0	0	0	0	0	0	0	0	0	0%
Item 14		0	0	0	0	0	0	0	0	0	0	0	0%
Total Category 4	0	0	0	0	0	0	0	0	0	0	0	0	0%
Total Expenses	0	0	0	0	0	0	0	0	0	0	0	0	0%
Operating Income													
Operating Income	0	0	0	0	0	0	0	0	0	0	0	0	0%
as a % of Revenue	0%	0%	0%	0%	0%	0%	0%	0%	0%	0%	0%		0%

Submitted by: _____   Date Updated: _____

UNDERSTANDING FINANCE

Breakeven Analysis Worksheet

Use this tool to determine a breakeven volume, the point at which total contribution equals fixed costs for your initiative. This will be calculated automatically as you enter your fixed costs, variable costs, and pricing information below.

Period: _____

Product: _____

Fixed Costs/Investment

Item 1

Item 2

Item 3

Item 4

Item 5

Item 6

Item 7

Item 8

Total Fixed Costs/Investment: | $0.00 |

Variable Costs per Unit

Item 1

Item 2

Item 3

Item 4

Item 5

Item 6

Item 7

Item 8

Total Fixed Costs/Investment: | $0.00 |

Unit Revenue:

Unit Contribution:

Breakeven Volume/

Incremental Volume Required: | $0.00 |

Notes:

Initiative Proposal Worksheet

Use this form to develop a proposal for an investment or another initiative.

Initiative Name:	Date:
Proposed By:	Status:

Description of Initiative

Rationale for Initiative

Initiative Economics

Component	Amount	Description
One-time investment		
Annual costs		
Annual revenues		
Annual savings		
Return on investment		
Payback period		
Other		

Nonmonetary Costs	*Nonmonetary Benefits*
Component	Component

Risk Factors

Factor	How Managed

Initiative Schedule

Target start date: _____   Target completion date: _____

Timing rationale: _____

Key Dates or Milestones	Deliverables	Key Dates or Milestones	Deliverables

Approved: _____   Date: _____

Pro Forma Financial Package (Introduction)

Contents

Overview

Planning for the future is something managers spend much of their time doing. Marketing plans new products, manufacturing plans material requirements, and finance plans how much money the company needs to operate from day to day. This is where financial forecasting comes in. When a company runs out of money, there is nothing it can do, short of winning the lottery, to sustain itself over the long run. By developing pro forma financial forecasts, managers can estimate their financing requirements and make plans accordingly. Through financial modeling, managers construct "what-if" scenarios by changing model inputs and observing the results, for better or worse. The pro forma model tool helps you build and analyze companies using this approach.

One major use of pro forma forecasting is estimating the future external financing needs of a company. This allows managers to seek out the necessary cash inflows before they impact normal company operations. There are several methods of forecasting financial statements, one of which is the percent-of-sales method. This simple but effective approach involves tying many of the income statement and balance sheet figures to future sales. This system works well because many of the variable costs and most current assets and liabilities vary more-or-less directly with sales. There are exceptions to this rule, but for our purposes (and this model) many of the line items take their cues from the annual growth in sales revenues.

The goal of this tool is to show you an example of a simple pro forma income statement, balance sheet, and cash flow analysis for a business. The results will be simple; for more advanced forecasting, you may need to adopt a more sophisticated financial planning tool. However, this tool will help you develop a solid initial understanding of the economics of a business and forecasting in general.

Before you begin, take a few minutes to look at the financial package as a whole. We've provided some sample data to give you a feel for how your results might look when you're done.

Tool Elements

Base Year

This is the starting point for entering data about the company you are analyzing. The model assumes that we are starting a new company; however, the base year can represent the company's first year in existence or the last year of actual data. The rest of the numbers are estimates of the first-year financials.

Assumptions

This tool includes an extensive list of assumptions for the model.

Income Statement - Balance Sheet - Cash Flow

These are the primary output reports of our base year and assumption inputs.

Income Statement Chart - Balance Sheet Chart
Cash Flow Chart - Cumulative Free Cash Flow Chart

These charts reflect the output on each of the associated reports.

Pro Forma Financial Package (Base Year)

Enter data in thousands of dollars

Base Year	2009

Income Statement

Revenue	2,000
Annual Revenue Growth Rate	20%
Total Cost of Goods Sold	900
Gross Margin	1,100
Sales Expenses	300
Marketing Expenses	100
General and Admin. Expenses	100
Other Expenses 1	0
Other Expenses 2	0
Other Expenses 3	0
Other Expenses 4	0
Total Operating Expenses	500
Depreciation Assumption	5 Year—Straight Line
Depreciation Expense	200
Operating Profit	400
Other Income (Expense)	0
Interest Income	3
Interest Expense	16
Pre-Tax Income	387
Income Tax Rate	20%
Income Tax	77
Net Income	310
Preferred Dividends	0
Common Dividends	0

Balance Sheet

As of	12/31/09
Assets	
Operating Cash	50
Marketable Securities	60
Accounts Receivable	80
Inventory	40
Other Current Assets	100
Total Current Assets	330
Gross Plant & Equipment	1,000
Accumulated Depreciation	100
Net Plant & Equipment	900
Other Long-Term Assets	100
Total Long-Term Assets	1,000
Total Assets	1,330
Liabilities	
Accounts Payable	50
Short-Term Debt	80
Current Maturities	15
Taxes Payable	5
Other Current Liabilities	40
Total Current Liabilities	190
Long-Term Debt	120
Term of Long-Term Debt	8 Years
Other Long-Term Liabilities	65
Total Long-Term Liabilities	185
Preferred Stock	0
Common Surplus	455
Retained Earnings	0
Shareholders Equity	455
Total Liabilities and Shareholders' Equity	830

Cash Flow Analysis

Capital Expenditures	500
Interest Income Rate	5%
Interest Expense Rate (Short-Term)	8%
Interest Expense Rate (Long-Term)	7%

Pro Forma Financial Package (Assumptions)

	Base Year	Year 1	Year 2	Year 3	Year 4	Year 5
	2009	2010	2011	2012	2013	2014
Annual Revenue Growth Rate		20.0%	20.0%	20.0%	20.0%	20.0%
Revenue	2,000	2,400	2,880	3,456	4,147	4,977
Cost of Goods Sold as a % of Revenue	45.0%	45.0%	45.0%	45.0%	45.0%	45.0%
Sales Expenses	15.0%	15.0%	15.0%	15.0%	15.0%	15.0%
Marketing Expenses	5.0%	5.0%	5.0%	5.0%	5.0%	5.0%
General and Admin. Expenses	5.0%	5.0%	5.0%	5.0%	5.0%	5.0%
Other Expenses 1	0.0%	0.0%	0.0%	0.0%	0.0%	0.0%
Other Expenses 2	0.0%	0.0%	0.0%	0.0%	0.0%	0.0%
Other Expenses 3	0.0%	0.0%	0.0%	0.0%	0.0%	0.0%
Other Expenses 4	0.0%	0.0%	0.0%	0.0%	0.0%	0.0%
Other Income (Expense) as a % of Revenue	0.0%	0.0%	0.0%	0.0%	0.0%	0.0%
Interest Income Rate	5.0%	5.0%	5.0%	5.0%	5.0%	5.0%
Interest Expense Rate (Short-Term)	8.0%	8.0%	8.0%	8.0%	8.0%	8.0%
Interest Expense Rate (Long-Term)	7.0%	7.0%	7.0%	7.0%	7.0%	7.0%
Income Tax Rate	20.0%	20.0%	20.0%	20.0%	20.0%	20.0%
Preferred Dividend Rate	0.0%	0.0%	0.0%	0.0%	0.0%	0.0%
Common Dividend Payout Ratio	0.0%	0.0%	0.0%	0.0%	0.0%	0.0%
Operating Cash as a % of Revenue	2.5%	2.5%	2.5%	2.5%	2.5%	2.5%
Accounts Receivable as a % of Revenue	4.0%	4.0%	4.0%	4.0%	4.0%	4.0%
Days Receivable	15	15	15	15	15	15
Inventory as a % of Cost of Goods Sold	4.4%	4.4%	4.4%	4.4%	4.4%	4.4%
Inventory Days	16	16	16	16	16	16
Other Current Assets as a % of Revenue	5.0%	5.0%	5.0%	5.0%	5.0%	5.0%
Capital Expenditures	500	380	452	546	667	822
Other Long-Term Assets as a % of Revenue	5.0%	5.0%	5.0%	5.0%	5.0%	5.0%

continued

Tools—Understanding Finance **143**

	Base Year	Year 1	Year 2	Year 3	Year 4	Year 5
	2009	2010	2011	2012	2013	2014
Accounts Payable as a % of COGS	5.6%	5.6%	5.6%	5.6%	5.6%	5.6%
Days Payable	20	20	20	20	20	20
Short-Term Debt	80	80	80	80	80	80
Current Maturities of Long-Term Debt	15	15	15	15	15	15
Long-Term Debt	120	105	90	75	60	45
Taxes Payable as a % of Taxes	6.5%	6.5%	6.5%	6.5%	6.5%	6.5%
Other Current Liabilities as a % of Revenue	2.0%	2.0%	2.0%	2.0%	2.0%	2.0%
Other Long-Term Liabilities as a % of Revenue	3.3%	3.3%	3.3%	3.3%	3.3%	3.3%
Preferred Stock	0	0	0	0	0	0
Common Surplus	455	455	455	455	455	455

Depreciation Tables: Assumes: 5 Year—Straight Line

Year	Capital Expenditures	Base Year	1	2	3	4	5	6
1	380			76	76	76	76	76
2	452				90	90	90	90
3	546					109	109	109
4	667						133	133
5	822							164
Depreciation for the Year			200	236	286	356	449	573
Net Plant & Equipment		900	1,080	1,296	1,555	1,866	2,239	0

Pro Forma Financial Package (Income Statement)

Data shown in thousands of dollars

	Base Year	Year 1	Year 2	Year 3	Year 4	Year 5
	2009	2010	2011	2012	2013	2014
Revenue	2,000	2,400	2,880	3,456	4,147	4,977
Cost of Goods Sold	900	1,080	1,296	1,555	1,866	2,239
Gross Margin	1,100	1,320	1,584	1,901	2,281	2,737
Sales Expenses	300	360	432	518	622	746
Marketing Expenses	100	120	144	173	207	249
General and Admin. Expenses	100	120	144	173	207	249
Other Expenses 1	0	0	0	0	0	0
Other Expenses 2	0	0	0	0	0	0
Other Expenses 3	0	0	0	0	0	0
Other Expenses 4	0	0	0	0	0	0
Total Operating Expenses	500	600	720	864	1,037	1,244
Depreciation Expense	200	236	286	356	449	573
Operating Profit	400	484	578	681	795	920
Other Income (Expense)	0	0	0	0	0	0
Interest Income	3	2	0	1	8	20
Interest Expense	16	28	33	19	12	11
Pre-Tax Income	387	458	545	663	791	929
Income Tax	77	92	109	133	158	186
Net Income	310	366	436	530	633	743
Preferred Dividends	0	0	0	0	0	0
Common Dividends	0	0	0	0	0	0

Pro Forma Financial Package (Balance Sheet)

Data shown in thousands of dollars

	Base Year	Year 1	Year 2	Year 3	Year 4	Year 5
	2009	2010	2011	2012	2013	2014
Assets						
Operating Cash	50	60	72	86	104	124
Marketable Securities	60	0	0	39	273	541
Accounts Receivable	80	96	115	138	166	199
Inventory	40	48	58	69	83	100
Other Current Assets	100	120	144	173	207	249
Total Current Assets	330	324	389	505	833	1,212
Net Plant & Equipment	900	1,080	1,296	1,555	1,866	2,239
Other Long-Term Assets	100	120	144	173	207	249
Total Long-Term Assets	1,000	1,200	1,440	1,728	2,074	2,488
Total Assets	1,330	1,524	1,829	2,233	2,906	3,701
Liabilities						
Accounts Payable	50	60	72	86	104	124
Short-Term Debt	80	80	80	80	80	80
Current Maturities	15	15	15	15	15	15
Taxes Payable	5	6	7	9	10	12
Other Current Liabilities	40	48	58	69	83	100
Total Current Liabilities	190	209	232	259	292	331
Long-Term Debt	120	105	90	75	60	45
Other Long-Term Liabilities	65	78	94	112	135	162
Total Long-Term Liabilities	185	183	184	187	195	207
Surplus Liabilities	0	311	157	0	0	0
Preferred Stock	0	0	0	0	0	0
Common Surplus	455	455	455	455	455	455
Retained Earnings	0	366	802	1,332	1,965	2,708
Shareholders' Equity	455	821	1,257	1,787	2,420	3,163
Total Liabilities & Shareholders' Equity	830	1,524	1,829	2,233	2,906	3,701
In-Balance Test	500	0	0	0	0	0

Pro Forma Financial Package (Cash Flow)

Data shown in thousands of dollars

	Base Year	Year 1	Year 2	Year 3	Year 4	Year 5
	2009	2010	2011	2012	2013	2014
Revenues	2,000	2,400	2,880	3,456	4,147	4,977
Earnings Before Interest & Taxes	400	484	578	681	795	920
Less Tax Exposure	80	97	116	136	159	184
Earnings Before Interest & After Taxes	320	387	462	545	636	736
Plus Depreciation	200	236	286	356	449	573
Operating Cash Flow	520	623	748	901	1,085	1,309
Operating Working Capital	175	210	252	302	363	436
Less Increase (Decrease) in Operating Working Capital	0	35	42	50	61	73
Plus Increase (Decrease) in Other Long-Term Liabilities	0	13	16	19	22	27
Less Increase (Decrease) in Other Long-Term Assets	0	20	24	29	35	41
Less Capital Expenditures	500	380	452	546	667	822
Free Cash Flow	20	201	246	295	346	400
Less After-Tax Interest Expense (Income)	10	21	26	15	4	(7)
Less Amortization of Debt	15	15	15	15	15	15
Less Total Dividends	0	0	0	0	0	0
External Financing Surplus (Deficit)		165	205	265	327	392

Pro Forma Financial Package (Income Statement Chart)

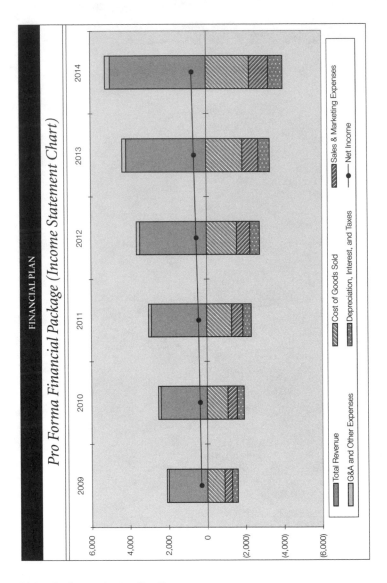

Pro Forma Financial Package (Balance Sheet Chart)

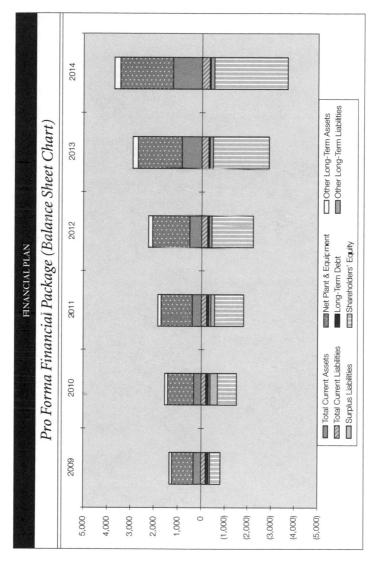

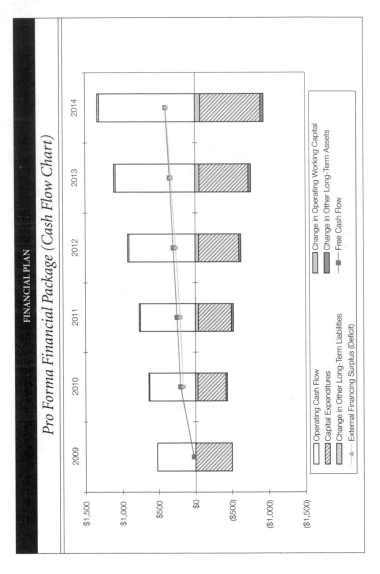

FINANCIAL PLAN

Pro Forma Financial Package (Cash Flow Chart)

Pro Forma Financial Package (Cumulative Free Cash Flow Chart)

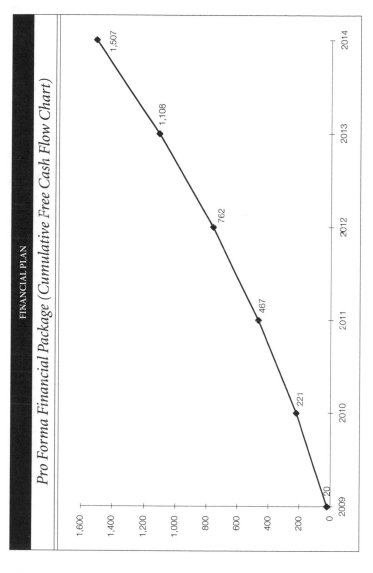

Test Yourself

This section offers ten multiple-choice questions to help you identify your baseline knowledge of finance essentials. Answers to the questions are given at the end of the test.

1. If you want to recognize revenue during the period in which the related sales activity occurred, which accounting method would you use?

   a. Accrual accounting.

   b. Cash-basis accounting.

2. Which of the following would be considered a cost of goods sold?

   a. Administrative employee salaries.

   b. Sales and marketing costs.

   c. Rents.

   d. Assembly labor costs.

   e. Advertising costs.

3. In most finance systems, what is the time frame that distinguishes short-term liabilities, also known as current liabilities, from long-term liabilities?

    a. Short-term liabilities typically have to be paid in a year or less; long-term liabilities take more than a year to repay.

    b. Short-term liabilities typically have to be paid within eighteen months; a long-term liability takes more than eighteen months to repay.

    c. Short-term liabilities typically must be paid in six months or less; long-term liabilities take over six months to repay.

4. If the income statement can tell you whether a company is making a profit, what does the cash flow statement tell you?

    a. How efficiently a company is using its assets.

    b. Whether a company is turning profits into cash.

    c. How well a company is managing its liabilities.

5. Many analysts like to look at a ratio that shows how profitable a company's operating activities are. Which ratio shows this?

    a. Acid-test ratio.

    b. Accounts receivable.

    c. EBIT margin.

6. At ABC Company, unit heads develop budgets for their departments that are linked to company performance objectives. Is this top-down or bottom-up budgeting?

a. Top-down.

b. Bottom-up.

7. As you begin to prepare your unit's budget, your manager reminds you to be aware of the "scope" of your budget. What does "scope" of a budget imply?

   a. The context of the proposed budget: the three to five goals that the budget you are going to prepare aims to achieve.

   b. The part of the company the budget is supposed to cover and the level of detail it should include.

   c. Whether the budget includes revenues and profits as well as the operating costs of your unit.

8. When you're preparing a cost/benefit analysis, net return and payback period analyses can help you compare and communicate the merits of different options. What, however, is the drawback to both analytic methods?

   a. Both net return and payback period analysis ignore the time value of money.

   b. Payback period and ROI do not take into account how long it will take for the investment to break even.

   c. ROI and payback period can only be used to evaluate potential capital investments, not other types of new business opportunities.

9. Your company is considering making an investment that could enable your division to sell more units of the Gargoyle tracking software introduced last year. Your manager has asked you to determine how likely it is that this investment will be recouped. What analytical method might give you this information?

   a. Sensitivity analysis.

   b. Breakeven analysis.

   c. Internal rate of return analysis (IRR).

10. To track your budget, you carry out three steps on a monthly basis. Step 2 is missing in the list below; what is it?

Step 1. Assess monthly revenue performance versus budget.

Step 2. _____

Step 3. Determine whether—and if so, how—your bottom line will be affected by any variances.

   a. Assess monthly expense performance versus budget.

   b. Assess monthly expense performance versus revenue performance for that same month.

   c. Compare monthly revenue performance with projected quarterly revenue performance.

Answers to test questions

1, a. With accrual accounting, income and expenses are recorded when they are incurred, regardless of whether cash is actually received or paid in that period. By matching revenues with expenses in the same time period, accrual accounting helps managers understand the true cause-and-effect connections between business activities.

2, d. Assembly labor costs are considered a "cost of goods sold." Cost of goods sold includes the materials, labor, and other expenses that are directly attributable to manufacturing a product or delivering a service.

3, a. Generally, short-term liabilities have to be paid in a year or less. Long-term liabilities stretch out over a longer time period and include items such as long-term bonds and mortgages.

4, b. It is the cash flow statement that tells you whether a company is turning its profits into cash.

5, c. Many analysts use the EBIT (earnings before interest and taxes) margin, often known as the operating margin, to see how profitable the company's operating activities are.

6, a. In top-down budgeting, senior management sets specific performance objectives for individual units. For instance, unit managers may be asked to limit expense growth to no more than 5 percent over last year's expenses. Unit managers then develop their budgets within those parameters to ensure that the high-level company objectives are achieved.

7, b. Scope implies two things: the part of the company your budget is supposed to cover and the level of detail it should include.

8, a. Because both methods ignore the time value of money, they do not provide as accurate an economic picture as more sophisticated tools, such as net present value and internal rate of return.

9, b. Breakeven analysis tells you how much (or how much more) of a product you need to sell in order to pay for a fixed investment—in other words, at what point you will financially break even. You can then use your sales history and knowledge of the market to determine whether the breakeven volume is achievable.

10, a. Step 2 is to assess the monthly expense performance versus budget. By understanding how revenue and expense performance compare against your budget, you can then determine whether (and how) your bottom line will be affected by any variances.

Key Terms

Accounts payable (A/P). Money owed by the firm to suppliers.

Accounts receivable (A/R). Money owed to a company for goods or services sold.

Accrual accounting. An accounting method whereby revenue and expenses are booked when they are incurred, regardless of when they are actually received or paid. Revenues are recognized during the period in which the sales activity occurred; expenses are recognized in the same period as their associated revenues.

Accruals. An amount incurred as an expense in a given accounting period—but not paid by the end of that period.

Acid-test ratio. See *quick ratio.*

Activity-based costing (ABC). An approach to cost accounting that focuses on the activities or cost drivers required to produce each product or provide each service. ABC assumes that most overhead costs are related to activities within the firm and that they vary with respect to the drivers of those activities.

Allocation. The process of spreading costs in a certain category to several cost line items, typically based on usage. For example, such corporate overhead expenses as rent and utilities may be charged to departmental units based on square feet.

Amortized expenses. The amount that is expensed over time for "soft" assets such as patents. They are expenses that are spread out over time to reflect their usable life.

Assets. The economic resources of a company. Assets commonly include cash, accounts receivable, notes receivable, inventories, land, buildings, machinery, equipment, and other investments.

Asset turnover. A measure of how efficiently a company uses its assets. To calculate asset turnover, divide sales by assets. The higher the number, the better.

Balance sheet. A means of summarizing a company's financial position—its assets, liabilities, and equity—at a specific point in time. According to the basic equation in a balance sheet, a company's assets equal its liabilities plus owners' equity. Balance sheet data is most helpful when compared with information from a previous year.

Banker's ratio. See *current ratio*.

Book value. The value at which an asset is carried on a balance sheet. The book value of equipment is reduced each year for depreciation. Therefore, the book value at any time is the cost minus accumulated depreciation.

Bottom-up budgeting. A process whereby managers put together budgets that they feel will best meet the needs and goals of their respective departments. These budgets are then "rolled up" to create an overall company budget, which is then adjusted, with requests for changes being sent back down to the individual departments.

Breakeven. The volume level at which the total contribution from a product line or an investment equals total fixed costs. To calculate the breakeven volume, subtract the variable cost per unit from the selling price to determine the unit contribution; then divide the total fixed costs by the unit contribution.

Capital expenditure/capital investment. The payment required to acquire or improve a capital asset. See *investment in PP&E.*

Cash-basis accounting. An accounting process that records transactions when cash actually changes hands. This practice is less conservative than accrual accounting when it comes to expense recognition, but sometimes more conservative when it comes to revenue recognition.

Cash flow statement. A review of a company's use of cash, this statement tells where the company's cash comes from and where it goes—in other words, the flow of cash in, through, and out of the company.

Chart of accounts. A way to outline a company's accounting system, the chart of accounts shows what information will be captured and what information will subsequently be readily retrievable by the system. The chart includes such items as inventory, fixed assets, accounts receivable, and costs.

Contributed capital. Capital received in exchange for stock.

Contribution. The unit revenue minus variable costs per unit. The sum of money available to contribute to paying fixed costs.

Cost/benefit analysis. A form of analysis that evaluates whether, over a given time frame, the benefits of the new investment or the new business opportunity outweigh the associated costs.

Cost of capital. The rate of return that a business could earn if it chose another investment with equivalent risk; also called opportunity cost.

Cost of goods sold (COGS). The costs directly associated with making and selling a product.

Cost of services (COS). The costs directly associated with developing and selling a service.

Costs and expenses. The costs related to running the business—for example, salaries, office overhead, light, heat, and legal and accounting services.

Current assets. Those assets that are most easily converted into cash: cash on hand, accounts receivable, and inventory.

Current ratio. This is a prime measure of how solvent a company is. It's so popular with lenders that it's sometimes called the *banker's ratio*. Generally speaking, the higher the ratio, the better financial condition a company is in. A company that has $3.2 million in current assets and $1.2 million in current liabilities would have a current ratio of 2.7 to 1. That company would be generally healthier than one with a current ratio of 2.2 to 1. To calculate the current ratio, divide total current assets by total current liabilities.

Days inventory. A measure of how long it takes a company to sell the average amount of inventory on hand during a given period of time. The longer it takes to sell the inventory, the greater the likelihood that it will not be sold at full value—and the greater the sum of cash that gets tied up. To calculate days inventory, divide average inventory by cost of goods sold per day.

Days payables. A measure that tells how many days it takes, on average, for a company to pay its suppliers. To calculate days payables, divide ending accounts payable by cost of goods sold per day.

Days receivables. A measure that tells you how long it takes, on average, for a company to collect what it is owed. A company that takes forty-five days to collect its receivables will need significantly more working capital than one that takes four days to collect. To calculate days receivables, divide ending accounts receivable by revenue per day.

Debt. What is owed to a creditor or supplier.

Debt to equity. This measure provides a description of how well the company is making use of borrowed money to enhance the return on owners' equity. To calculate the debt-to-equity ratio, divide total liabilities by total shareholders' equity.

Depreciation. A way of matching the cost of capital expenditures to the revenue it helps bring in.

Direct versus indirect costs. Costs that are directly attributable to the manufacture of a product—for example, the cost of plastic for a bottling company. Direct costs vary in direct proportion to the number of units produced. Indirect costs cannot be directly attributed to a particular product.

Dividend. A payment (usually occurring quarterly) to the stockholders of a company, as a return on their investment.

Earnings before interest and taxes (EBIT). See *operating profit.*

Earnings per share (EPS). One of the most commonly watched indicators of a company's financial performance, it equals net income divided by the number of shares outstanding. When EPS falls, it usually takes the stock's price down with it.

Earnings statement. See *income statement.*

Economic Value Added (EVA). The profit left over after a company has met the expectations of those who provided the capital.

Equity. The value of a company's assets minus its liabilities. On a balance sheet, equity is referred to as *shareholders' equity* or *owners' equity.*

Financial leverage. A company's long-term debt in relation to its capital structure (the total of its common stock, preferred stock, long-term debt, and retained earnings). A company that has consistently high earnings can afford to be more leveraged; that is, it can afford to carry more long-term debt than a company whose earnings fluctuate significantly.

Financial statements. Reports of a company's financial performance. The three basic types of statement included in an annual report—the *income statement,* the *balance sheet,* and the *cash flow statement*—present related information but provide different perspectives on a company's performance.

Fiscal periods. An accounting time period (month, quarter, year), at the end of which the books are closed and profit or loss is determined.

Fixed assets. Assets that are difficult to convert to cash—for example, buildings and equipment. Sometimes called long-term assets.

Fixed costs. Fixed costs remain constant despite sales volume; they include interest expense, rent, depreciation, and insurance expenses.

General ledger. A company's centralized and authoritative accounting record, where data included in the financial statements is detailed.

Generally accepted accounting principles (GAAP). The rules and conventions that accountants follow in recording and summarizing transactions and preparing financial statements.

Gross margin. A ratio that measures the percentage of gross profit relative to revenues.

Gross profit. The sum left over after you subtract COGS from revenue.

Growth. An increase in the company's revenues, profits, or the value of its equity.

Growth indicators. Measures that tell about a company's financial health. Common measures of growth include sales growth, profitability growth, and growth in earnings per share.

Hurdle rate. The rate of return on investment dollars required for a project to be worthwhile.

Income statement. A report that shows a company's revenue, expenses, and profit over a period of time—a month, a quarter, or a year. The income statement is also known as a profit and loss statement (P&L), statement of operations, and statement of earnings. It also can have the word *consolidated* in the title.

Interest coverage. This measures a company's margin of safety, or how many times over the company can make its interest payments. To calculate interest coverage, divide income before interest and taxes by interest expense.

Internal rate of return (IRR). The rate at which the net present value (NPV) of an investment equals zero.

Inventory. The assets of the company that are or will become its product. Examples include the merchandise in a shop, the finished work in a warehouse, work in progress, and raw materials.

Investment in PP&E. Dollars spent on property, plant, and equipment. Sometimes called *capital investment* or *capital expenditure.*

Invoice. A bill submitted to the purchaser, listing all items or services, together with amounts for each.

Journals. The transaction records of the business.

Leverage ratios. Ratios that tell you about a company's use of debt. These ratios, including *interest coverage* and *debt to equity*, help determine whether a company's level of debt is appropriate and assess its ability to pay the interest on its debts.

Liabilities. The economic claims against a company's resources. Such debts include bank loans, mortgages, and accounts payable.

Net book value (NBV). The value at which an asset appears on the books of an organization, minus any depreciation (usually as of the date of the last balance sheet) that has been applied since its purchase or its last valuation.

Net income. The profit of an organization after subtracting all expenses, including interest and taxes, from revenue.

Net income per employee. See *productivity measures.*

Net present value (NPV). The value of an investment, calculated by subtracting the cost of the investment from the present value of the investment's future earnings. Because of the time value of money, the investment's future earnings must be discounted in order to be expressed accurately in today's dollars.

Net profit margin. See *return on sales.*

Net return. A ratio measuring the value of the returns from an investment relative to its cost.

Operating cash flow (OCF). The net movement of funds from the operations side of a business, as opposed to cash from investing or cash from financing. OCF is usually described in terms of the sources and uses of cash. When more cash is going out than coming in, there is a negative cash flow; when more cash is coming in than going out, there is a positive cash flow.

Operating expenses. Expenses that occur in operating a business—for example, administrative employee salaries, rents, sales and marketing costs, as well as other costs of business not directly attributed to manufacturing a product.

Operating profit. The profit left over after subtracting the costs and expenses associated with conducting business from revenue. Also known as *earnings before interest and taxes (EBIT)*.

Operating ratios. Financial measures that link various income statement and balance sheet figures to provide an assessment of a company's operating efficiency. Examples of operating ratios include *asset turnover*, *days receivables*, *days payables*, and *days inventory*.

Owners' equity. See *equity*.

Payback period. The length of time needed to recoup the cost of a capital investment; the time that transpires before an investment pays for itself.

Pretax profit. Net income before federal income taxes.

Price-to-book ratio. A ratio comparing the market's valuation of a company to the value of that company as indicated on its financial statements.

Price-to-earnings ratio (P/E). A common measure of how cheap or expensive a stock is, relative to earnings. P/E equals the current price of a share of stock divided by the previous twelve months' earnings per share.

Productivity measures. Indicators such as sales per employee and net income per employee, which link revenue and profit generation information to workforce data, thereby providing a picture of which employees are producing the most sales and income.

Profitability ratios. Measures of a company's level of profitability, in which sales and profits are expressed as a percentage of various other items. Examples include *return on assets*, *return on equity*, and *return on sales.*

Property, plant, and equipment (PP&E) A line item on a balance sheet that lists the purchase price of the business's land, buildings, machinery, equipment, and natural resources that are used for the purpose of producing products or providing services.

Purchase order. A written authorization to a vendor to deliver goods or services at an agreed-upon price. When the supplier accepts the purchase order, it is a legally binding purchase contract.

Quick ratio. A measure of a company's assets that can be quickly liquidated and used to pay debts. It is sometimes called the *acid-test ratio*, because it measures a company's ability to deal instantly with its liabilities. To calculate the quick ratio, divide cash, receivables, and marketable securities by current liabilities.

Ratio analysis. A means of analyzing the information contained in the three financial statements, a financial ratio is two key numbers from a company's financial statements expressed in relation to each other. Ratios are most meaningful when compared with the same measures for other companies in the same industry.

Retained earnings. The total after-tax income that has been reinvested over the years of the business.

Return on assets (ROA). Expressed as a percentage, ROA is a quantitative description of how well a company has invested in its assets. To calculate it, divide the net income for a given time period by the total assets. The larger the ROA, the better a company is performing.

Return on equity (ROE)/return on owners' equity. This measure shows the return on the portion of the company's financing that is provided by owners. To calculate ROE, divide the total income by total owners' equity.

Return on sales (ROS). Also known as *net profit margin*, ROS is a way to measure a company's operational efficiency—how its sales translate into profit. To calculate ROS, divide net income by the total sales revenue.

Sales. An exchange of goods and services for money.

Shareholders' equity. See *equity*.

Sunk costs. Prior investment that cannot be affected by current decisions and thus should not be factored into the calculation of the profitability of an initiative.

SWOT analyses. An analysis of a company's strengths, weaknesses, opportunities, and threats.

Time value of money. The principle that a dollar received today is worth more than a dollar received at a given point in the future. Even without the effects of inflation, the dollar received today would be worth more because it could be invested immediately, thereby earning additional revenue.

Top-down budgeting. A budgeting process whereby senior management sets very specific objectives for such things as net income, profit margin, and expenses. Unit managers then allocate their budget within these parameters to ensure that the objectives are achieved.

Valuation. An estimate of a company's value, usually for the purposes of purchase and sale. Wall Street uses valuation to describe a company's financial performance in relation to its stock price: *earnings per share (EPS)*, *price-to-earnings ratio (P/E)*, and *price-to-book ratio.*

Variable costs. Costs that are incurred in relation to sales volume; examples include the cost of materials and sales commissions.

Working capital. A measure of a company's day-to-day liquidity, working capital equals the difference between a company's current assets (easily sellable goods, cash, and bank deposits) and its current liabilities (debt due in less than a year, interest payments, etc.). Shortages of working capital are often relieved by short-term loans.

To Learn More

Notes and Articles

Hawkins, David F., and Jacob Cohen. "The Balance Sheet." Note 9-101-108. Boston: Harvard Business School, 2001.

Discusses the accounting equation and defines common terms found in the statement. Also provides an example of the balance sheets of Coca-Cola Co., Ariba, Inc., and Safeway, Inc.

Hawkins, David F., and Jacob Cohen. "The Statement of Cash Flows." Note 9-101-107. Boston: Harvard Business School, 2001.

Discusses the components of the statement of cash flows and its direct and indirect format of presentation. Also briefly explains the difference between cash and accrual accounting and provides examples of Standard Microsystems Corp. and Intel Corp.

Kaplan, Robert S., and David P. Norton. "The Balanced Scorecard: Measures That Drive Performance." *Harvard Business Review* On-Point Enhanced Edition (2000).

The balanced scorecard performance measurement system allows executives to view a company from several perspectives simultaneously. The scorecard includes financial measures that reveal the results of actions already taken, as well as three sets of operational measures that assess customer satisfaction, internal processes, and the organization's ability to learn and improve.

Books

Berman, Karen, Joseph V. Knight, and John Case. *Financial Intelligence: A Manager's Guide to Knowing What the Numbers Really Mean.* Boston: Harvard Business School Press, 2006.

In *Financial Intelligence*, Berman, Knight, and Case teach the basics of finance—but with a twist. Financial reporting, they argue, is as much art as science. Because nobody can quantify everything, accountants always rely on estimates, assumptions, and judgment calls. Savvy managers need to know how those sources of possible bias can affect the financials and that sometimes the numbers can be challenged. While providing the foundation for a deep understanding of the financial side of business, the book also arms managers with practical strategies for improving their companies' performance—strategies, such as "managing the balance sheet," that are well understood by financial professionals but rarely shared with their nonfinancial colleagues. Accessible, jargon-free, and filled with entertaining stories of real companies, *Financial Intelligence* gives nonfinancial managers the financial knowledge and confidence for their everyday work.

Bruns, William J., Jr., Michael E. Edelson, Steve R. Foerster, W. Carl Kester, Timothy A. Luehrman, Scott P. Mason, David W. Mullins Jr., Andre F. Perold, and William A. Sahlman. *Finance for Managers.* Business Fundamentals Series. Boston: Harvard Business School Press, 1999.

This collection introduces managers to basic financial tools and concepts. Topics addressed include short- and long-term financial management, investment management, risk management, and valuation. It contains materials used in Harvard Business School's MBA and executive education programs. Includes the following items: "Note on the Financial Perspective: What Should Entrepreneurs Know?" by William A. Sahlman; "Note on Financial Programming Over Long Horizons" by Timothy A. Luehrman; "Introduction to Portfolio Theory" by Andre F. Perold; "Basic Capital Investment Analysis" by William J. Bruns Jr.; and "What's It Worth? A General Manager's Guide to Valuation" by Timothy A. Luehrman.

Jablonsky, Stephen F., and Noah P. Barsky. *The Manager's Guide to Financial Statement Analysis.* 2nd ed. New York: John Wiley & Sons, 2001.

This book is for nonfinancial managers who want to learn the language of business finance and accounting in order to become more effective in their jobs. Supplemented with several case studies of major corporations, the author explains how to get the most out of the complicated information provided in balance sheets, income statements, and other sections of the annual report, as well as in the *Wall Street Journal, Value Line,* and *BusinessWeek.*

Kaplan, Robert S., and David P. Norton. *The Strategy-Focused Organization: How Balanced Scorecard Companies Thrive in the New Business Environment.* Boston: Harvard Business School Press, 2000.

The creators of the revolutionary performance management tool called the Balanced Scorecard introduce a new approach that makes strategy a continuous process owned not just by top management, but by everyone. Kaplan and Norton articulate the five key principles required for building strategy-focused organizations: (1) translate the strategy into operational terms, (2) align the organization to the strategy, (3) make strategy everyone's everyday job, (4) make strategy a continual process, and (5) mobilize change through strong, effective leadership. The authors provide a detailed account of how a range of organizations in the private, public, and nonprofit sectors have deployed these principles to achieve breakthrough, sustainable performance improvements.

Sources

We would like to acknowledge the sources who aided in developing this topic.

Bruns, William J., Jr. "The Accounting Framework, Financial Statements, and Some Accounting Concepts." Note 9-193-028. Boston: Harvard Business School, 1993.

Bruns, William J., Jr. "A Brief Introduction to Cost Accounting." Note 9-192-068. Boston: Harvard Business School, 1993.

Bruns, William J., Jr. "Introduction to Financial Ratios and Financial Statement Analysis." Note 9-193-029. Boston: Harvard Business School, 1996.

Dickey, Terry. *The Basics of Budgeting.* Menlo Park, CA: Crisp Publications, 1992.

Hindle, Tim, chief contributor, and Alistair D. Williamson, ed. *Field Guide to Business Terms: A Glossary of Essential Tools and Concepts for Today's Manager.* The Economist Reference Series. Boston: Harvard Business School Press, 1993.

Livingstone, John Leslie, ed. *The Portable MBA in Finance and Accounting.* 2nd ed. New York: John Wiley & Sons, 1997.

Schleifer, Arthur, Jr. "Breakeven Analysis." Note 9-894-002. Boston: Harvard Business School, 1995.

Tracy, John A. *Budgeting à la Carte: Essential Tools for Harried Business Managers.* New York: John Wiley & Sons, 1996.

Tracy, John A. *The Fast Forward MBA in Finance.* New York: John Wiley & Sons, 1996.

Wilson, G. Peter. "Understanding the Statement of Cash Flows." Note 9-193-027. Boston: Harvard Business School, 1992.

Tools and Resources for Preparing a Budget

Budget Preparation and Tracking

Use this worksheet to prepare and track an annual budget needed for your department, division, or business unit.

	Q1 budget	Q1 actual	Q2 budget	Q2 actual	Q3 budget	Q4 actual	Q4 budget	Q4 actual	YTD budget	YTD actual	YTD difference	YTD % difference
Revenues (list sources on separate lines)												
Total revenues												
Expenses (list items on separate lines)												
Total expenses												
Operating income as a % of revenue												

Submitted by:

Date updated:

Budget Preparation Checklist

Use this form to identify sources of information for your budget. You can change the items listed to fit your situation, such as a service business or start-up company.

Revenue   *Do you have information from or about:*

☐ Senior management, goals and objectives, strategy, mission
☐ Sales and marketing managers' projections, marketplace data, goals
☐ Current levels of sales
☐ Incremental changes

☐ Industry predictions/expectations, trends
☐ Field sales representatives' projections, marketplace data, assessment of competition
☐ Other: for example, new technology's impact

Production Costs   *Do you have information from or about:*

Direct Materials

Current Costs

☐ Incremental change
☐ Suppliers; their predictability to deliver

☐ Purchasers estimates/expectations
☐ Industry predictions

Direct Labor

☐ Contractual changes
☐ Expected outsourcing

☐ Expected contract changes
☐ Expected overtime

☐ Changing requirements
☐ Human resource predictions

Direct Manufacturing

Variable Costs

☐ Supplies
☐ Maintenance
☐ Power

Fixed Costs

☐ Depreciation
☐ Property taxes
☐ Insurance
☐ Supervision

Do you have information from or about:

- ☐ Incremental change
- ☐ Suppliers' estimates/expected changes
- ☐ Purchasers estimates/expectations
- ☐ Industry predictions

Nonproduction Costs *Do you have information from or about:*

Variable Costs

- ☐ R&D/product design
- ☐ Marketing/Advertising
- ☐ Customer Service
- ☐ Administration
- ☐ Distribution

Fixed Costs

- ☐ R&D/product design
- ☐ Marketing/Advertising
- ☐ Customer Service
- ☐ Administration
- ☐ Distribution

Do you have information from or about:

- ☐ Incremental change
- ☐ Suppliers' estimates/expected changes
- ☐ Purchasers estimates/expectations
- ☐ Industry predictions

Cash Budget

Use this worksheet to calculate your cash requirements by quarter.
Enter your detailed estimates of cash receipts and disbursements
in the spaces provided, or add new lines.

Cash Budget for Fiscal Year

	Quarters				Year Totals
	1	2	3	4	
Cash balance, beginning					
Add receipts					
Cash sales					
Collections from accounts receivable					
Investment income					
Total cash available for needs (a)					
Deduct disbursements					
Direct materials					
Payroll					
Income taxes					
Other costs					
Machinery purchase					
Total disbursements (cash needed) (b)					
Cash excess (deficiency) (a) – (b)					
Financing					
Borrowing (at beginning)					
Repayment (at end)					
Interest on borrowing					
Total effects of financing (d)					
Cash balance, ending (a) – (b) + (d)					

(Continued)

Test Yourself

This section offers ten multiple-choice questions to help you identify your baseline knowledge of the essentials of preparing a budget. Answers to the questions are given at the end of the test.

1. Which of the following is *not* a true statement?

a. A budget is an action plan for allocating resources and expenditures.

b. A budget is a historical record of a company's financial results.

c. A budget is a yardstick for measuring managers' performance.

2. The most important element of the budget-preparation process is:

a. The assessment of variances between expected and actual results.

b. The communication and planning that occur in preparing a budget.

c. The end result—the operating, capital, or cash budget that is created.

3. One significant disadvantage associated with zero-based budgeting is:

  a. Its in-depth analysis.

  b. Its overall inaccuracy.

  c. Its time costs.

4. An expense that stays the same when there is an increase in the volume of product produced is categorized as a:

  a. Fixed cost.

  b. Variable cost.

  c. Constant cost.

5. Your company's marketing department is forecasting a 15 percent increase in sales revenue next year. What assumptions should you, the production department manager, make from this forecast as you prepare your budget for next year?

  a. Sales volume will increase 15 percent.

  b. No assumptions can be made from this forecast.

  c. Sales volume will remain the same next year.

6. It is October 1, and your department's year-to-date revenue is 20 percent less than what you had budgeted year-to-date. The run rate has jumped sharply since July, while your total expenses are right on budget. One-half of your annual bonus depends on achieving budgeted revenues by the end of the year and one-half on achieving budgeted gross margin. What action should you take?

- a. Reduce prices and increase spending on advertising and marketing.
- b. Increase prices as well as spending on advertising and marketing.
- c. Examine expense items to see whether there are any adjustments to spending you should make.

7. Capital budgeting is the process of:

- a. Identifying the potential return on a given investment to determine whether the investment makes sense and to compare alternative investment options.
- b. Estimating future outlays for property, equipment, and capital assets.
- c. Plotting the expected cash balances that the organization will experience during the forecast period.

8. You want to determine the potential impact on your division's operating income if the number of product units sold increases by 10 percent, if the number of product units sold decreases by

5 percent, and if material costs decrease by 5 percent. What would you do?

    a. Estimate costs associated with expected revenues (the cost of goods sold and the estimated SG&A), and calculate expected operating income.

    b. Differentiate between fixed and variable costs, and then allocate costs using activity-based costing (ABC).

    c. Conduct a sensitivity analysis comparing the units sold, material costs, and operating income shown in your budget against those you would see under the three proposed scenarios.

9. Which of the following goals might be appropriate for the vice president of purchasing?

    a. Reduce material costs by 15 percent.

    b. Reduce overhead by 10 percent.

    c. Increase sales revenue by 10 percent.

10. True or false: the balanced scorecard is linked to the budget process by highlighting the financial results that the company intends to achieve through its competitive strategy.

    a. True.

    b. False.

Answers to test questions

1, b. A budget is *not* a historical document but rather a forward-looking action plan that guides managers' allocation of resources and expenditures based on their assumptions about the future.

2, b. The planning and communication activities that take place in formulating a budget require managers to consider longer-term goals, challenges, and opportunities facing the organization—all of which shape major decisions about how to respond.

3, c. One problem that occurs with zero-based budgeting is that the time involved in the budget-preparation process can overwhelm planners, making implementation difficult. Managers have to balance the need for increased accuracy with the time required to collect further information.

4, a. Fixed costs, such as rent, administrative costs, and insurance, do not vary with incremental changes in production volumes.

5, b. Before you can make assumptions that inform your own budget, you must identify the assumptions behind the marketing department's revenue forecast. For example, the marketing manager may assume that the projected growth in revenue will come from a lower selling price and a dramatic increase in volume; a higher selling price and a decline in the number of units sold; or a jump in sales volume due to other factors, such as increased spending on advertising. Each of these assumptions will have different implications for your budget. Only after you've clarified marketing's assumptions can you then begin preparing your own budget.

6, c. The rising run rate indicates that sales are increasing. And if this continues, sales may come in on budget by the end of the year. The greater risk, and one over which you have more control, is that you will not meet the budgeted gross margin unless you reduce expenses to match the shortfall in revenue.

7, a. Capital budgeting involves evaluating the financial soundness of a proposed capital investment and choosing among alternatives.

8, c. A sensitivity analysis applies a "what-if" situation to the budget model to see the effect of the potential change on the original data. Using sensitivity analysis, you can see the possible impact of a change in your assumptions, without having to generate new forecasts for each budget item, such as raw materials.

9, a. The purchasing department can make a significant contribution to reducing materials costs by controlling what the company pays for raw materials, and packaging.

10, b. The balanced scorecard does not favor the financial perspective; rather, it is linked to the budget process by (1) highlighting leading indicators; (2) balancing the financial, customer, internal process, and innovation and improvement perspectives; and (3) helping managers communicate strategic goals to all stakeholders.

Key Terms

Activity-based budgeting (ABB). A form of budgeting based on activity-based costing (ABC) that focuses on the cost of the activities involved in all functional areas of an organization.

Activity-based costing (ABC). A process by which managers identify the cost of resources, allocate these costs to activities, and then allocate the cost of activities to products.

Allocated costs. Non-production-related costs—such as rent, insurance, and administrative costs—that are allocated to individual units' operating budgets based on that unit's output.

Balanced scorecard. A method of translating an organization's strategic mission into multiple and linked objectives, focusing on financial, customer, internal business, and innovation and learning perspectives.

Budget. An organization's action plan, translating strategic objectives into measurable quantities that express the expected resources required and returns anticipated over a certain period of time.

Capital budget. A schedule detailing planned investment in capital assets, property, and equipment.

Capital budgeting. A method of evaluating investment proposals to determine whether they are financially sound, and to allocate limited capital resources to the most attractive proposals.

Cash budget. A plan or schedule for expected cash inflows and outflows.

Financial budget. The part of the master budget that includes the budgeted balance sheet, the capital budget, the cash budget, and the budgeted statement of cash flows. The financial budget describes the expected sources of capital required to support the operating budget.

Fixed budget. A budget in which the amounts are fixed over the budget period.

Fixed costs. Costs that remain the same through a wide range of production and sales volumes.

Flexible budget. A budget that can be "flexed" or adjusted when variances are computed to recognize the actual revenues and costs.

Gross margin. Gross profit divided by total revenue. Gross profit is total revenue minus cost of goods sold.

Incremental budgeting. A method of budgeting in which data from historical figures is used to establish a basis for future assumptions.

Kaizen budgeting. A form of budgeting that strives for continuous cost improvement or reduction.

Master budget. The umbrella budget that summarizes and integrates all the individual budgets within an organization.

Net present value. The current value of a future stream of cash flows, based on specific interest rate assumptions.

Operating budget. The part of the master budget that includes the expected revenues and costs summarized in the budgeted income statement.

Operating income. Revenue less cost of goods sold and selling, general, and administrative costs.

Participatory budgeting. A budgeting approach that incorporates input from line managers in formulating assumptions and goals.

Revenue per employee. A measure of productivity, calculated by dividing total revenues by the number of full-time employees.

Rolling budget. A plan that is continually being updated so that the budget time frame remains stable while the actual periods covered by the budget change. At the end of each period (month, quarter, or year), a future period is added to the budget.

Run rate. An estimate of a future cost or revenue amount based solely on the current cost or revenue level.

SG&A. Selling, general, and administrative costs.

Static budget. A budget that remains unchanged throughout the budget period based on one set of expected outputs. Variances are computed at the end of the budget period.

Top-down budgeting. A budgeting approach in which individual departmental goals are set by senior management.

Variable costs. Costs that fluctuate with incremental changes in output.

Variance. The difference between an actual amount and a budgeted amount in a financial budget plan.

Zero-based budgeting. The method of beginning each new budgeting process from a zero base, or from the ground up, as though the budget were being prepared for the first time. Every assumption and proposed expenditure receives a critical review.

To Learn More

Articles

Boesen, Thomas. "New Tools for a New Corporate Culture: The Budget-less Revolution." *Balanced Scorecard Report*, January 2002.

Borealis, Europe's leading polyolefin plastics manufacturer, replaced its traditional budget process with four core management systems, including the balanced scorecard. In a Q&A with the *Balanced Scorecard Report*, Thomas Boesen, the company's former financial controller, describes the new budgeting and planning approach. One by-product of the new program: four systems focused on the company's different needs eliminated much of the complexity, confusion, and inflexibility of the old budgeting system.

Gary, Loren. "Breaking the Budget Impasse." *Harvard Management Update*, May 2003.

Has your company's budget process helped you do a better job of belt-tightening during the current slowdown? Chances are that it hasn't. You hate the entire budget process, and you never see it pay off. So why do you keep doing it the same old way? Read what the experts have to say about not only changing your budgeting process, but whether your company should dispense with budgets entirely. The reality is that your budgeting process should be a tool for achieving strategic alignment, not for driving you insane.

Horvath, Peter, and Ralf Sauter. "Why Budgeting Fails: One Management System Is Not Enough." *Balanced Scorecard Report*, September 2004.

It's inefficient, ages too quickly, and is out of sync with the strategic plan. No wonder so many executives hate toiling over the annual budget. But, says Peter Horvath (Europe's leading authority on management accounting, controlling, and budgeting), don't look to the budget as the sole management system. Horvath and his associate Ralf Sauter describe six ways to fix budgeting, including integrating it with such systems as the balanced scorecard, so that it supports strategy execution in today's fast-changing environment.

Kaplan, Robert S., and David P. Norton. "The Balanced Scorecard: Measures That Drive Performance." *Harvard Business Review* On-Point Enhanced Edition, February 2000.

Kaplan and Norton developed a "balanced scorecard" performance measurement system that allows executives to view a company from several perspectives simultaneously. The scorecard includes financial measures that reveal the results of actions already taken, as well as three sets of operational measures that show customer satisfaction, internal processes, and the organization's ability to learn and improve. Creating a balanced scorecard requires translating a company's strategy and mission statement into specific goals and measures. Managers then track those measures as they work toward their goals.

Kaplan, Robert S., and David P. Norton. "Linking Strategy to Planning and Budgeting." *Balanced Scorecard Report*, May 2000.

Kaplan and Norton show how traditional budgeting practices can be made more responsive to a company's rapidly changing needs. They urge managers not just to focus on the operational budget, but to pay attention to the strategy budget as well, because that's what finances the initiatives that facilitate company growth. Managers also need to avoid falling into the trap of thinking that initiatives are ends in themselves. Rather, initiatives are the means by which a company accomplishes its strategic objectives.

Norton, David P., and Philip W. Peck. "Linking Operations to Strategy and Budgeting." *Balanced Scorecard Report*, September 2006.

In part 1 of this two-part series, Linking Strategy and Planning to Budgets, David P. Norton made the case for a new expense category, STRATEX, dedicated to funding strategic initiatives—the means by which the enterprise carries out strategy. In part 2, Norton and Philip W. Peck argue that successful strategy execution requires more than just a separate strategy budget: the organization must link both strategy and operations to the budget—and do so in a way that is transparent (thus easy to analyze and revise) and future focused. Causal models, driver-based planning, and adaptive tools such as rolling forecasts together constitute just such an integrating mechanism that can also give organizations more information (the whys, not just the whats), flexibility, and agility—vital capabilities in a competitive, fast-changing world.

Wardell, Charles. "High-Performance Budgeting." *Harvard Management Update*, January 1999.

No one looks forward to the budgeting process. It's most often viewed as an unproductive exercise that steals time from your real job. However, the budget can be a powerful instrument for helping with forecasting, planning, and employee involvement. To accomplish this, you must first reengineer the budgeting process. Then you have to rethink how you use the budget itself. The traditional budget and the budgeting process are not adequate for today's economy. Some key flaws are the inability to quantify significant metrics such as innovation and quality and the tendency to compartmentalize a company into small units, providing departments with no incentive to look at the big picture. *HMU* presents a new approach to budgeting by offering a six-point checklist that shows how to turn your budgeting process, and the resulting budget, into powerful tools.

Books

Harvard Business School Publishing. *Harvard Business Essentials Guide to Finance for Managers*. Boston: Harvard Business School Press, 2002.

Calculating and assessing the overall financial health of the business is an important part of any managerial position. From reading and deciphering financial statements, to understanding net present value, to calculating return on investment, *Finance for Managers* provides the fundamentals of financial literacy. Easy to use and nontechnical, this helpful guide gives managers the smart advice they need to increase their impact on financial planning, budgeting, and forecasting.

Hope, Jeremy, and Robin Fraser. *Beyond Budgeting: How Managers Can Break Free from the Annual Performance Trap.* Boston: Harvard Business School Press, 2004.

The traditional annual budgeting process—characterized by fixed targets and performance incentives—is time consuming, overcentralized, and outdated. Worse, it often causes dysfunctional and unethical managerial behavior. Based on an intensive, international study into pioneering companies, *Beyond Budgeting* offers an alternative, coherent management model that overcomes the limitations of traditional budgeting. Focused around achieving sustained improvement relative to competitors, it provides a guiding framework for managing in the twenty-first century.

Kaplan, Robert S., and David P. Norton. *The Strategy-Focused Organization: How Balanced Scorecard Companies Thrive in the New Business Environment.* Boston: Harvard Business School Press, 2000.

In this book, Kaplan and Norton describe how the concept of the balanced scorecard has progressed beyond its original usefulness as a tool to measure performance to a way of actually effecting strategic change. Using examples drawn from company experiences, the authors show how the balanced scorecard can help the strategy-focused organization achieve nonlinear performance breakthroughs.

Simons, Robert. *Performance Measurement and Control Systems for Implementing Strategy.* Upper Saddle River, NJ: Prentice Hall, 2000.

Simons presents a coherent body of practical theory that shows how new accounting and control tools can be used to implement strategy. He shows how techniques for performance measurement and control, aligning performance goals and incentives, and managing strategic risk can be implemented by managers to achieve profit goals and strategies.

Sources

The following sources aided in development of this book:

Harvard Business School Publishing. "High-Performance Budgeting." *Harvard Management Update*, January 1999.

Harvard Business School Publishing. "Preparing a Budget." *Harvard ManageMentor* eLearning program, Personal Insight.

Horngren, Charles T., George Foster, and Srikant M. Datar. *Cost Accounting: A Managerial Emphasis.* Upper Saddle River, NJ: Prentice Hall, 1997.

Kaplan, Robert S., and Robin Cooper. *Cost and Effect: Using Integrated Cost Systems to Drive Profitability and Performance.* Boston: Harvard Business School Press, 1998.

Kaplan, Robert S., and David P. Norton. "The Balanced Scoreboard—Measures That Drive Performance." *Harvard Business Review*, January–February 1992.

Kaplan, Robert S., and David P. Norton. *The Strategy-Focused Organization: How Balanced Scorecard Companies Thrive in the New Business Environment.* Boston: Harvard Business School Press, 2001.

Marks, Eileen R., associate publisher, Harvard Business School Publishing. Personal conversation, fall 2000.

Narayanan, V. G., associate professor, Harvard Business School. Personal conversations, fall 2000.

Simons, Robert. *Performance Measurement and Control Systems for Implementing Strategy.* Upper Saddle River, NJ: Prentice Hall, 2000.

About the Subject Experts

Karen Berman, Subject Expert, Understanding Finance

Karen Berman, PhD, is founder, president, and co-owner of the Business Literacy Institute, a consulting firm offering customized training programs, Money Maps, keynotes, and other products and services designed to ensure that everyone in organizations understands how financial success is measured and how they make an impact. Karen has worked with dozens of companies, from enterpreneurial firms to *Fortune* 500 organizations, helping them create financial literacy programs that transform employees, managers, and leaders into business partners. She is also coauthor, along with Joe Knight, of *Financial Intelligence: A Manager's Guide to Knowing What the Numbers Really Mean* (Harvard Business School Press, 2006).

Chuck Kremer, Subject Expert, Understanding Finance

Chuck Kremer, CPA, has many years' experience as an accountant, corporate controller, and business consultant. He is currently the senior business-literacy consultant with Novations VMS. He has helped thousands of nonfinancial executives overcome "fear of finance" using imaginative and enjoyable devices in Novations' *Financial Game for Decision Making* and *The Accounting Game* seminars. He is the lead coauthor of *Managing by the Numbers: A Commonsense Guide to Understanding and Using Your Company's Financials.* Chuck has developed *The Financial Scoreboard*, an Excel software template.

Linda A. Cyr, Subject Expert, Financial Plan

Linda A. Cyr is a partner at Tapestry Networks, a company that brings leaders together for strategic dialogues that set the agenda for economic, social, and organizational change. Linda's career spans both academic and corporate settings. Most recently, Linda was an assistant professor at the MIT Sloan School of Management and the Harvard Business School, where she created and taught entrepreneurship and leadership courses for both MBA students and executives. Her research and teaching examined ways in which a company's network of internal and external affiliations affects its financial performance. She has published articles in *The Academy of Management Journal* and *Entrepreneurship Theory and Practice* in addition to authoring Harvard Business School cases spanning industries that include biotech, consumer products, technology, and fashion.

V. G. Narayanan, Subject Expert, Preparing a Budget

V. G. Narayanan teaches both basic and advanced courses in financial and accounting topics to MBA and doctoral students at Harvard Business School, where he is the Thomas D. Casserly Jr. Professor of Business Administration. He believes that budgets must accomplish more than control purposes to serve an organization well. He consults with numerous businesses and has a special interest in managerial accounting. V. G. has contributed articles to accounting journals and has published many case notes for the school. He is a graduate of Stanford University, where he received his MS in statistics, MA in economics, and PhD in business. His ability to make difficult concepts comprehensible is evidenced in this topic on budgeting, which has a practical approach.